· WARD LOCK MASTER GARDENER ·

Growing Indoor Pla

JANE COURTIER

WARD LOCK

First published in Great Britain in 1993
by Ward Lock Limited, Villiers House, 41/47 Strand,
London WC2N 5JE, England
A Cassell Imprint

British Library Cataloguing in Publication Data
is available upon application to the British Library

ISBN 0-7063-7106-2

Text filmset by RGM Associates, Southport
Printed and bound in Singapore

Previous page: **A diverse collection of foliage plants shows the wide range of colour, shape and texture that exists.**

Page 4: **Foliage plants brighten our rooms throughout the year, but are particularly appreciated during the winter months.**

Contents

Preface

There is so much pleasure to be gained from sharing our homes and workplaces with plants. The fresh living green of foliage, with its multitude of different shapes and textures; the unfolding flowers in their range of colours and fragrances – they serve to remind us of the natural world that sometimes seems so far away from our finely controlled, often artificial modern environments.

Indoor plants need our care to thrive; there is nothing more disappointing than watching a beautiful new purchase fade and die before our eyes. Most plants are not difficult to keep; it is often simply a lack of understanding of their particular needs that leads to failure.

This book aims to help you choose your plants wisely and care for them well, catering for all their needs, protecting them from pests and diseases, and even raising new plants to increase your stock.

Indoor plants are well worth a little time and trouble. They will more than repay you with many months or even years of pleasure.

J.C.

ACKNOWLEDGEMENTS

The publishers are grateful to the following for granting permission to reproduce the following colour photographs: Photos Horticultural Picture Library (front cover main photograph, pp. 16 (upper), 17, 21, 41, 52, 60, 61, 64, 68, 72, 73, 76, 77, 84, 85, 88 & 93); Pat Brindley (pp. 1, 8, 12, & 49 (lower)); Harry Smith Horticultural Photographic Collection (pp. 9, 16 (lower), 37, 45, 49 (upper), 53, 57 & 81); *Amateur Gardening* magazine (pp. 13, 20, 24, 25, 29, 32 (both), 36, 44, 65 & 89).

The photographs on pp. 92 & 93 were taken by Clive Nichols and Ed Gabriel respectively.

The line drawings were drawn by Vana Haggerty F.L.S. and Nils Solberg.

·1·
The Value of Indoor Plants

Plants don't just belong in the garden – think how long we have used them to brighten our homes and offices. There is nothing like a fresh growing plant to cheer up sometimes rather sterile and artificial surroundings.

Although the use and range of indoor plants has increased quite dramatically in recent years, the idea is by no means new. Since the first greenhouses were constructed in the sixteenth century, exotic plants have been nurtured in otherwise unsuitable climates and, long before that, plants were being grown in containers for decorative purposes. They would not have been limited to wealthy households: I'm sure that hard-working cottagers would have found it difficult to resist the temptation to dig up a few primrose plants and place them in some suitable containers of soil on their windowsills as a living proof of the arrival of a long-awaited spring. Now we no longer have to dig up plants from outside: any garden centre or high street florists' will provide us with an amazing selection of flowers and foliage.

But buildings can provide a hostile environment for plants. The low light levels and warm, dry air often mean that plants don't thrive as they would in their natural environment outdoors, and they can need careful attention. On the other hand, protection from harsh weather has given us the opportunity to grow and admire exotic, foreign species that would not normally survive outside.

An indoor plant is simply one that will adapt to growing in an environment primarily constructed for people to live in. It does not have to be tender and fragile: many useful indoor plants (ivy, for example) are quite tough enough to cope with the worst that cold weather can throw at them. It does need, however, to be able to grow in a container in a reasonably small amount of soil or compost and to be fairly compact in growth. It does not need to be long-lived in these conditions: several popular house plants are short term, being discarded once they are past their best. Others can, with care, continue to flourish and give pleasure for many years.

Plants are completely different to other forms of decoration, such as ornaments and pictures. Every living plant is unique: there is no other one in the world that is exactly the same. A plant changes over the weeks and months, developing, growing, perhaps flowering and fruiting. It may mark the seasons, even in an artificial, centrally heated environment. A plant requires our care. It depends on us to survive, and gives us a sense of responsibility.

Perhaps most of all plants remind us of a more basic existence when all life revolved around growing crops and the changing seasons. In our high tech, finely controlled modern environments, many of us have lost touch with the earth as ultimate provider. Is it possible that the few

struggling cuttings growing in old yogurt pots on an office windowsill are the last enduring link with our agricultural heritage?

Indoor plants may be grown for their flowers (and sometimes fruits) or for their foliage, or occasionally for both.

Foliage

Foliage plants can be just as spectacular and striking as flowering types.

Foliage may be notable for its shape, colour or texture; individual leaves may be large and attractive, like the deeply cut foliage of the Swiss cheese plant (*Monstera deliciosa*) or they may give

an overall effect, like the feathery trails of asparagus fern (*Asparagus sprengeri*). The texture can vary from the amazing purple plush of the velvet plant (gynura) to the deeply crinkled *Peperomia caperata* or succulent, spiny-edged agaves (Fig. 1).

There are soft, gently flowing outlines and statuesque 'architectural' plants; climbers, scramblers and plants that grow to form robust indoor 'trees' (Fig. 2).

When it comes to colour, the choice is immense. There are dozens of different shades of green, from the dark foliage of the rubber plant (there is even a variety called 'Black Prince') to the fresh light

◀ An arrangement of mainly foliage plants shows a good contrast of leaf forms and colour, and is given extra emphasis by the addition of a colourful flowering hibiscus.

▶ Grouping plants together is a much more effective way of displaying them: the plants will also thrive in the humid microclimate that is produced.

green of tolmiea; then there are the variegated varieties, subtly or boldly marked with white, silver or gold, and sometimes also shades of pink, red and orange.

• *Variegated plants* have become increasingly popular, and there is a wide range of forms available. Sometimes just the margin of a leaf is picked out in a contrasting colour; this may be a fine edge, as on the thin leaves of *Dracaena marginata* which are delicately trimmed with red, or a broader, irregular band, as *Hedera canariensis* 'Gloire de Marengo', which has some leaves with the merest splash of green in the centre of a cream sea. Other variegations may be reversed – a green edge with a contrasting centre – or an all-over effect of mottling, marbling or striping. Scindapsus (devil's ivy or pothos) comes in a number of varieties with different variegations. *Scindapsus aureus* is green, streaked with gold, while the variety 'Golden Queen' is more gold streaked with green. 'Marble Queen' is a particularly beautiful variety, the leaves being white, lightly marked with light and deeper green.

Ficus benjamina, the lovely weeping fig, has creamy edged leaves in the form 'Variegata', but 'Starlight' has a more striking variegation with large patches of creamy white on the foliage. Apart from the different forms and varieties, the amount and type of variegation differs from plant to plant, so when buying, it pays to look through a batch of plants carefully to choose the one with the most attractive markings.

On some leaves, the veins are picked out in a different shade; the prominent white veins of aphelandra contrast with the deep green leaf to earn it its common name of zebra plant. The most popular of the marantas, *Maranta leuconeura erythrophylla* (more often known as 'Tricolor') has bold red veins, emphasized by the midrib being irregularly backed with yellow into the bargain.

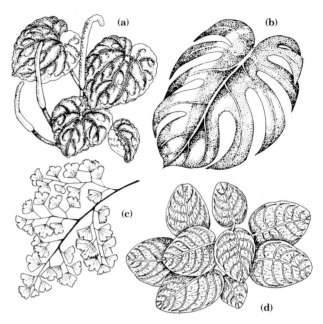

Fig. 1 Foliage varies dramatically from plant to plant: (a) deeply textured peperomia (b) large and boldly cut monstera (c) fragile, delicate maiden fern, and (d) strikingly patterned fittonia.

There are some amazingly delicate leaf markings. Calatheas (related to marantas) are sometimes called peacock plants, and one look at the intricate leaf patterns will tell you why. *Calathea makoyana* is probably the most attractive, its papery white leaves bearing a tracery of green veins and broader 'peacock's eyes'.

Even more delicate is caladium, or angels' wings. The large, arrow-shaped leaves are paper thin, almost translucent, coloured in a variety of shades of white, pink and green. The leaves are delicate, and so is the plant – not one of the easiest to keep, but certainly one of the most showy.

Joseph's coat was one of many colours, so you know what to expect from a plant with Joseph's coat as its common name. The croton, or codiaeum,

·HANDY TIP·

Clever lighting can turn a group of plants into a particularly striking feature at night. Try experimenting with spotlights and 'uplighters' to create different effects with shadows and highlights, but be careful not to position lamps too close to plants. Tungsten bulbs give off a lot of heat and could scorch foliage.

One group of plants has leaves which consist of radiating leaflets on top of a tall stalk: the group of leaflets looks a little like the spokes of an umbrella, which gives rise to common names such as umbrella plant and parasol plant. One of the easiest of all house plants comes into this group: it is cyperus, which grows quite happily in water. There are two types, both known as umbrella plant: *Cyperus diffusus* and *Cyperus alternifolius* which grows a little taller. It is impossible to overwater these plants, making them a popular choice for those people who can't seem to grow other house plants!

is a popular plant with large leaves, often irregularly shaped, marked with a variety of pinks, yellows and greens. This one could never be called subtle, but it is certainly eye-catching.

Even more brilliantly and extravagantly coloured is the easily grown coleus. This nettle-leaved plant, which is very easily raised from cuttings or seed, has leaves edged, streaked or blotched with a variety of fiery hues: brilliant reds, yellows and oranges as well as various shades of green. The margins of the leaves may be deeply indented or ruffled. These almost gaudy plants are one of the few foliage plants that have to be treated as temporary, for they soon grow unattractively leggy, but replacements are easily raised from soft tip cuttings.

• *Leaf shape* A lot of interest can be obtained from varying shapes of leaves. Palms give a tropical touch to rooms; there are many different varieties, all with divided leaves. These may be hand or fan shaped; the European fan palm (*Chamaerops humilis*) is one of the easiest fan palms to grow, but trachycarpus, washingtonia and livistona have similar fan-shaped leaves, sometimes with fibrous tips which add to their attraction. Feather palms have fronds which are divided into leaflets and include date palm (*Phoenix* species), the popular parlour palm, *Neanthe bella* and coconut palms (*Cocos* species).

Fig. 2 Shapes of plants include (a) the tree-like *Ficus benjamina* (b) trailers such as scindapsus and (c) the bushy dieffenbachia, while (d) mother-in-law's tongue is dramatically spiky.

The coppery coloured young foliage of dizygotheca (sometimes called aralia) is attractive: the most popular species is *Dizygotheca elegantissima*. The umbrellas of toothed leaflets give the plant a spidery appearance. Heptapleurum is available in a variegated form, heavily splashed with gold; the leaflets are wider than umbrella plants already mentioned. Schefflera has wide 'spokes', too, and will grow into an attractive specimen tree where it is happy.

Most people are familiar with the rubber plant, *Ficus elastica*, but a more spectacular leaf shape is provided by the fiddle-leaved fig, *Ficus lyrata*. Each leaf is shaped roughly like a violin, and is about the same size.

There are very many more aspects of foliage plants: some of the most popular varieties will be described later in this book, but look round any good garden centre and you will find a vast array of different sorts of leaves. For the most part, foliage plants give year-round interest. They remain indoors all the time; they do not need to spend the summer outside as some flowering plants do. They are, of course, mainly evergreen, and will continue

◄ Flowering bulbs make cheerful short-term room plants. They flower much earlier indoors than outside, even when not specially 'treated', bringing the promise of spring to winter days.

► A mixed group of flowering plants to give good winter colour. The hyacinths will not last as long as the chrysanthemums and pointsettias, but can be replaced as they fade.

in growth throughout the year provided temperature and light levels allow it. They are particularly valuable in the house because of their virtually permanent display.

Flowers

Flowering plants, by and large, have a shorter display season, though many have foliage which is pleasing enough to earn them a place indoors even when they are out of flower. Some types are easy to get to bloom, others much more of a challenge. Some plants just won't flower unless conditions are exactly right for them, but others will flower almost anywhere.

Flowers on house plants can be had in almost any colour you care to think of, and the range of shapes is surprising (Fig. 3). Flowers may be followed by

fruits, and these are often the main attraction. Some 'flowers' are not flowers at all; the popular poinsettia has quite insignificant flowers in the centre of its brilliantly coloured bracts (which are modified leaves), and the white 'bloom' of the peace lily (spathiphyllum) is really a spathe.

• *Scent* Some flowers have a magnificent scent. The waxy white flowers of stephanotis are often used in brides' bouquets, and their heavy, rich scent can fill a large room. The twining *Jasminum polyanthum* is rather easier to grow and has a lighter but still very strong and sweet perfume: genista (*Cytisus racemosus*) bears its bright yellow broom flowers in late winter, and has a spicy penetrating scent. Most of the indoor bulbs – hyacinths and narcissi, for example – are pleasantly scented, too.

• *Short-term plants* Some flowering indoor plants need to be treated as strictly temporary. While some just need to repair to a greenhouse or even a sheltered spot outdoors until they are ready to bloom again, others have little or no chance of making an attractive plant after their first flowering season is over, and should be discarded. Some receive special treatment from the producers which is difficult or even impossible to carry out in the home: dwarfing chemicals may be used to keep plants compact, or complex lighting regimes may need to be followed to bring plants into flower.

·SCENTED HOUSE PLANTS·	
Name	**Description**
Citrus	Strongly scented white flowers produced sporadically from spring to autumn
Cyclamen	Swept back flowers in a range of colours; light, delicate scent, particularly from miniature varieties variable from plant to plant – sniff out the best when buying!
Gardenia	Large, white, waxy flowers with a strong, penetrating, sweet fragrance
Hoya	Climbers or trailers with white, pink-centred waxy flowers, star-shaped with an intense, sweet perfume
Hyacinth	Various types suitable for forcing in winter; well-known, penetrating sweet scent which turns mushroomy as the flowers fade
Jasmine	Twiner with bunches of starry, white, scented winter flowers
Myrtle	White blooms with a brush of white stamens in the centre; fragrant leaves and flowers
Narcissus	Lots of fragrant varieties, but 'Paperwhite' is perhaps the best of all
Stephanotis	Trumpet-shaped, waxy white blooms on a twining plant; very strong perfume

Pot chrysanthemums, for example, will grow to their natural size of 1 m (3 ft) or more once they have used up all the chemical dwarfing compound in their compost; they would make ungainly room plants, though they can be planted out in the garden where they will grow like any normal outdoor perennial. Many people find it impossible to bring poinsettias into bloom again after their first Christmas, even if they are successful in keeping the plant alive. This is because flowering is initiated only when the hours of darkness are longer than the hours of daylight, and artificial lighting used indoors will trick the plant into thinking the correct season has not arrived, and prevent it forming its colourful bracts. Poinsettias are also treated with a dwarfing compound, so plants kept after their first year will cease to be compact and become rather leggy, though still manageable as a pot plant.

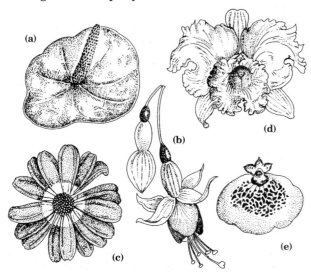

**Fig. 3 Some of the many flower shapes of indoor plants:
(a) palette-like anthurium (b) pendulous fuchsia bells
(c) cineraria 'daisies' (d) the exotic orchid and (e) pouch-shaped calceolaria.**

·ARCHITECTURAL PLANTS·

Name	Description
Chamaerops humilis (European fan palm)	Deeply cut, fan-shaped leaves up to 2 m (6½ ft), arising from stout, hairy trunks
Dracaena marginata (Madagascar dragon tree)	Can reach over 2 m (6½ ft), with long, narrow, red-edged sword-like leaves
Fatshedera lizei	Large, hand-like leaves; can be grown as a bush by pinching out the young shoots, or as a climber
Ficus benjamina (weeping fig)	Elegant weeping tree with many branches and small, shiny, pointed leaves; grows to about 2 m (6½ ft)
Ficus elastica 'Decora' (rubber plant)	Large, oval, shiny, deep green leaves on an upright plant that will reach 3 m (10 ft) when given the chance; tends to go bare at the base of the main stem; bright red bud sheaths
Ficus lyrata (fiddle-leaved fig)	Similar to the rubber plant but with large – up to 45 cm (18 in) long – leaves which have the shape of a violin
Howea forsteriana (Kentia palm)	Feathery leaves with long, arching leaflets arising on long stems from short trunks; slow growing up to 2 m (6½ ft) or more
Monstera deliciosa (Swiss cheese plant)	Large, shiny, deep green leaves which start off entire and gradually develop the characteristic 'holes' as they age; a scrambling plant that will grow up to 3 m (10 ft)
Philodendron bipinnatifidum	A non-climbing type with large, glossy green, lobed leaves that look rather like those of a Swiss cheese plant; will grow up to 2 m (6½ ft) but needs support
Schefflera actinophylla (umbrella plant)	Long leaflets arranged in 'spokes' at the tips of the leaf stalks on a plant that will grow up to 2 m (6½ ft)
Yucca elephantipes	A statuesque plant with long, sword-like leaves giving the appearance of a palm

15

▲ A mixture of plants in one container makes an attractive display. In time, the plants can be potted up separately as they are too crowded to thrive for long as a group.

► Mixing the levels when arranging a large group of plants gives a satisfying effect. Here the floor, a plant trough and the wall have all been put to good use.

Architectural plants

In large rooms, particularly, a striking focal point is sometimes needed, and here a so-called 'architectural' or specimen plant is required. These plants are often seen in the reception areas of offices and public buildings, where they create a pleasant but impressive environment.

Architectural plants are large and imposing, with an attractive overall shape. The indoor figs (*Ficus* family) provide some excellent specimens: a large and well-grown rubber plant (*Ficus elastica*) is often used, but even more popular now is the graceful tree shape of *Ficus benjamina*, the weeping fig. Some of the palms make good focal points, as does the sword-like mother-in-law's-tongue, particularly the golden-edged variety *Sansevieria trifasciata laurentii*.

When provided with firm supports, the climbing philodendrons and monsteras can make striking specimens, and the spiky dracaenas, yuccas and cordylines make dramatic, exotic looking 'trees'.

A focal point may also be made up of a group of plants, generally with a tree-like specimen to give height, some bushy, perhaps colourful-leaved varieties around the base, and trailers to soften the overall outline. All the plants used in the group must like the same sort of growing conditions, and preferably grow at the same rate. Sometimes certain plants need to be removed and replaced as they outgrow their space.

• *Specimen plant care* To be an effective focal point, a specimen plant must be large – and that generally means expensive. It must also be kept in first class condition, with healthy, glossy, deep green leaves. In public buildings, such plants are usually cared for by expert contractors, who take care to site plants properly, keep them correctly fed and watered, control pests and remove and replace any plants showing signs of stress. If you buy an expensive specimen plant for your home, you don't

This Kentia palm makes a striking 'architectural' plant, perfectly complementing the upright lines of the long-case clock.

have this sort of expert back-up, so it is vitally important that you choose a plant that is suited to the position you have in mind for it. The difficulty of looking after such plants is reflected in the fact that so many very realistic artificial plants are now available!

17

·2·
House Plant Care

Although plants vary in their individual requirements, they all have certain common needs. The basic requirements for growth are light, water, certain minerals and a degree of warmth. Most also require some form of support for their root systems.

Light

Green-leaved plants manufacture their own food supply by converting the energy of light into carbohydrates in their leaves. If insufficient light (or the wrong type of light) is available, leaves will turn yellow, growth will slow and plants will eventually die.

Light levels in rooms are dramatically lower than outside (which is why many plants placed on a windowsill will tend to have their leaves leaning towards the sunlight unless they are turned regularly – see Fig. 4). Many house plants adapt well to these conditions; in their natural habitat they may grow in shady forests, where they are never exposed to the sun. However, even though some plants require shading from direct sun, they may still need very bright conditions – a combination that is often difficult to achieve in the home. The quality of light entering a room also varies according to season, and the aspect of the windows (Fig. 5).

A garden room or conservatory, both of which have a much higher proportion of glass than a normal living room, will provide much better light conditions, and most plants will grow better there. Some form of shading will generally have to be provided, though, to protect foliage from scorching, as well as to prevent temperatures climbing too high.

Because the human eye is not very efficient at judging the quantity and quality of light, it is often a good idea to use a photographic light meter to give an accurate reading, especially in a house that is new to you.

Different plants have different light requirements, so selection can be made to suit different rooms and parts of rooms. If you know the natural origins of the plant, you will have a good idea of the light it is likely to require. Desert cacti, for example, would hardly be expected to be shade lovers, while ferns that grow in the deep, cool, woodland shade are unlikely to respond well to direct sun. Sometimes, however, varieties have been bred which do not have the same requirements as their natural parents, so this can be misleading.

Warmth

Some plants require warm conditions to survive; all require some degree of warmth in order to grow satisfactorily.

Plants that do best as indoor plants are those that like the same degree of warmth to live in as humans: this is generally around 20°C (68°F).

Some indoor plants, however, will survive frosts quite happily, while others will struggle to survive below 15°C (59°F).

Once the temperature drops below a certain level (the exact temperature varies from species to species), plant growth will stop. Some plants will shed their leaves and survive as a rootstock or dormant bulb, rhizome, etc.; others will just fail to make new growth. If freezing conditions occur, many house plants will be killed altogether. On others, the topgrowth may be killed while the rootstock survives. A few plants retain their foliage throughout freezing conditions.

Hand in hand with the temperature goes the humidity of the air – the amount of moisture it carries. Many plants can thrive in high temperatures as long as the atmosphere is moist. In dry conditions, however, leaves quickly begin to crisp up, and the plant shows signs of stress. The majority of indoor heating systems supply very dry air – not the best conditions for most plants. The level of humidity should always be borne in mind when choosing plants for certain temperature ranges.

Water

Water is necessary for several vital functions of plants, as it is for people. Water is usually taken up through the roots, though some plants absorb it through their leaves. Insufficient water often brings about an extremely rapid response from plants.

Water keeps plant cells turgid, thus keeping the plant in shape. When there is insufficient water, the plant tissues become flaccid; first the leaves droop and become soft, and then the non-woody stems. Wilting of the foliage is an obvious sign that the plant requires watering, but other, more subtle

▼ Fig. 4 A plant growing by a one-sided light source, such as a window, will grow towards the light. Regular turning would prevent the plant becoming lopsided.

► Fig. 5 Different parts of a room receive varying amounts of light. Plants need to be positioned with care, according to their light requirements.

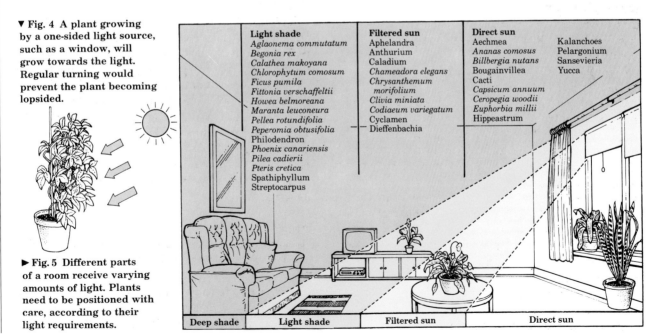

Light shade
Aglaonema commutatum
Begonia rex
Calathea makoyana
Chlorophytum comosum
Ficus pumila
Fittonia verschaffeltii
Howea belmoreana
Maranta leuconeura
Pellea rotundifolia
Peperomia obtusifolia
Philodendron
Phoenix canariensis
Pilea cadierii
Pteris cretica
Spathiphyllum
Streptocarpus

Filtered sun
Aphelandra
Anthurium
Caladium
Chameadora elegans
Chrysanthemum
  morifolium
Clivia miniata
Codiaeum variegatum
Cyclamen
Dieffenbachia

Direct sun
Aechmea   Kalanchoes
Ananas comosus   Pelargonium
Billbergia nutans Sansevieria
Bougainvillea   Yucca
Cacti
Capsicum annuum
Ceropegia woodii
Euphorbia millii
Hippeastrum

| Deep shade | Light shade | Filtered sun | Direct sun |

◄ Cacti are among the relatively few plants that will thrive in bright, direct sunlight. They also require less frequent watering than many other plants, and will soon suffer if overwatered.

► Not all plants need soil in which to grow. Tillandsias – air plants – live naturally on tree branches, and make attractive features when fixed to pieces of driftwood.

damage may often have been done before this stage is reached. Flower buds may drop before developing, leaves may fall, and growing tips may die back, even if the plant apparently recovers after watering.

Overwatering, which can easily occur in the relatively small volumes of compost potted plants grow in, floods the roots, depriving them of air. Roots then begin to die, leading to very similar symptoms to those of underwatering, but the state of the compost usually makes it obvious which complaint the plant is suffering from.

Different plants have different water requirements. Some, like cyperus, can live quite happily with their roots standing in water permanently. Others, like many succulents, are adapted to live in conditions of low water supply, and are soon killed by overwatering. The more actively a plant is growing, the greater its water needs will be.

21

Growing media

Plants need some substance from which to obtain their water and nutrients, and to give them support so that they can grow. For the majority of plants this is soil. Their root systems develop in the soil and spread outwards and downwards, absorbing nutrients and water; their shoots grow up through the soil surface and develop in the light and air.

Plants do not need soil in which to grow, however. A variety of substances have been used successfully: peat, rockwool, vermiculite, pebbles, Leca granules and others. For growing plants indoors, a clean, lightweight substance is preferred, and peat-based composts are understandably very popular. Alternatives to peat are being increasingly used. They are formulated to provide a similar type of compost to peat, though they are not identical.

Soils contain most of the mineral nutrients that plants need: man-made growing media do not. Nutrients have to be added by the manufacturers and later also supplied in the form of fertilizers by those who grow the plants.

Not all plants grow in soil. Air plants (tillandsias) have modified leaves that can absorb sufficient moisture and nutrients from the air: some bromeliads live on tree branches, and take in water and nutrients from the moisture that collects in the central funnels of their rosettes of leaves.

Nutrients

Plants manufacture their food source – carbohydrates – from light, but they also need certain other chemical nutrients in order to function. These are nitrogen, phosphorus and potassium, plus, in smaller amounts, minerals such as magnesium, manganese, iron and others. These are usually present in most soils in sufficient quantities, but some soils can become deficient in one or other of them, which gives rise to a range of symptoms. Yellowing foliage, or foliage with yellow veins of yellow markings between the veins, are frequent indicators of nutrient deficiency.

Rest periods

Some plants continue in growth throughout the year, provided light levels, water supply and temperatures are suitable. Others need a rest period, during which they cease to grow and become dormant, for their proper development.

Where light levels become weaker in winter, plants will not grow so rapidly as they do in summer, even if temperature, feeding and watering remain the same. Unless artificial light can be provided, feeding should be stopped, and the temperature and water supply should be reduced to equate with the reduced light level, so the plant is given a winter rest. Once light levels become stronger in spring, watering can be gradually increased, temperatures raised, and feeding can begin again.

CULTIVATION TECHNIQUES

Knowing the general requirements of plants, it is easier to set about providing them with suitable conditions in the home.

Watering

Incorrect watering must be the single most common cause of failure with indoor plants. The first rule is to know the water requirements of the particular plant you are growing. Some groups have very obvious preferences – desert cacti, for instance. But there are many indoor plants that are not so obvious in their needs, and while some do have distinct preferences for being kept very moist or rather dry, the majority require a compost that is kept just moist throughout the growing period, and allowed to dry out slightly in the 'dormant' season.

The best watering technique where the particular preference of a plant is not known is to wait until the surface of the compost in the pot is just dry to the touch, then water it thoroughly, standing the pot in a deep dish to catch the water

(a) Break up soil surface with fork to allow water to penetrate.

(b) Immerse pot in water until compost is thoroughly moistened, and spray foliage with hand sprayer.

Fig. 6 A complete collapse is often caused by the plant drying out – but symptoms of overwatering are identical. Check the state of the compost before watering.

that flows through the drainage holes. Allow the pot to remain standing in the water for no more than 20 minutes, then tip away the surplus water and leave the plant until the compost surface becomes dry again (Fig. 6).

When plants are known to like moist conditions, the surface of the compost need not be allowed to dry out before rewatering, but care must be taken not to saturate the compost (except for one or two plants that do not mind this). If a plant prefers to be kept on the dry side, allow the compost to become dry a little further down the pot before watering; stop watering once water begins to flow through the drainage holes and do not leave it to stand in the water at all.

Plants require more regular watering when they are growing strongly, in early and mid-summer. When growth starts to slow down in autumn, gradually reduce the watering.

Feeding

Plants should normally be fed only when they are growing strongly, in spring and summer. When they are newly potted in fresh compost, they do not need feeding straight away: there are sufficient nutrients in the compost to keep them going. After a few weeks or months, the nutrients in the compost will begin to run out; peat-based composts become exhausted more quickly than soil-based types. The plant may start to look a little dull and lifeless, with smaller, not so deeply coloured leaves; its rate of growth may slow down considerably.

There are various types of fertilizer suitable for house plants. Probably the most popular is liquid fertilizer. Liquid fertilizers are diluted and applied to the compost when it is already moist – there is a risk of scorching the roots if they are applied when the compost is dry. They are generally applied fortnightly, depending on the formulation and the type of plants being fed.

Slow-release fertilizers are applied as granules once a year, ideally in spring. A combination of warmth and moisture breaks down the granules so that the fertilizer content is gradually released over a long period – ideal for people who don't want to bother with frequent feeding.

There are also fertilizers formulated as solid spikes or tablets to be pushed into the compost at the edge of the pot. These last for around two months, and can be used in spring or summer. Different brands have different fertilizer formulations – for flowering plants and for foliage plants, for example.

Foliar feeds are the fastest acting of all fertilizers. They are sprayed directly on to the leaves, where they are rapidly absorbed to give a very quick response. Not all fertilizer formulations can be absorbed properly by leaves; it is important to use those specially designed for the job, which will not scorch the foliage. It is important to dilute foliar feeds according to the instructions on the pack when making up a solution. Foliar feeds often contain trace elements – nutrients which are required in tiny quantities but can often be deficient in composts – because this is a particularly good way of getting the plant to absorb them. Foliar feeds should not be sprayed on to flowers, in direct sunlight, or on to some delicate and hairy-leaved plants.

Providing warmth

Although 20°C (68°F) might be the average preferred temperature for people's living conditions, this is not always the temperature in homes and workplaces. In winter, only a few rooms in a house may be heated: those that are not frequently used may be very cold. Rooms that are used for relaxing, where not much activity is taking place to keep the occupants warm, can easily reach 27°C (80°F) and above when the heating is on.

Some situations may fluctuate widely: a workplace may maintain a temperature of 24°C (75°F) from Monday to Friday, but when the heating is switched off at the weekend, it may drop to 4°C (39°F) or below. As a general rule, indoor plants have to put up with the temperatures that suit the other inhabitants; rooms are rarely heated to suit the plants.

Try to provide plants with as even a temperature as possible. They should not be situated directly against or above a heat source such as a radiator, nor should they be positioned in a draught.

A deep windowsill which is cut off from the rest of the room by curtains or blinds at night can become

▲ Foliar feeds, sprayed directly on to leaves, are the fastest acting of all fertilizers. They must be correctly formulated for this type of feeding or leaf scorch could result.

▶ Supplementary lighting helps keep plants growing through the winter. Special plant growth bulbs are available, or fluorescent light bulbs can be used.

very cold. This is not a position for your most delicate and temperature-sensitive plants unless they are brought into the room when the curtains are drawn.

A number of indoor plants find heated living rooms too warm for comfort. Cape heaths (*Erica hyemalis*) are extremely difficult to keep alive for more than a few weeks, and cyclamen soon become drawn and unattractively leggy. The place for these types of plant is somewhere cooler, such as a well-lit hallway.

Don't forget about plants requiring humidity along with heat. One of the best ways to provide this is to group plants on a large tray of pebbles which extends well under all the foliage. Keep the tray nearly topped up with water (making sure the bases of the pots are standing on the pebbles and not actually in the water). Many plants also enjoy being misted with a fine spray of plain water from a hand sprayer.

Pruning and training

Dead and dying foliage, stems and flowers should always be removed cleanly and destroyed: you may need a sharp knife or secateurs for this. Left on the plant, they may provide an entry point for fungal diseases.

Many plants need regular pinching of the growing tips to keep them shapely. Fast-growing plants such as coleus and bloodleaf (iresine) soon become ungainly if they are not regularly pinched to stimulate the production of side shoots. There is no need to pinch back too hard – just remove the soft, growing tip.

Climbers and trailers, too, need some gentle pinching to keep them in line; they may also need to be trained on to some form of support. This might be trelliswork fixed to a wall, or a moss pole, or wire hoop, or any number of types of support placed in the pot. Some plants will cling to their supports or twine round them themselves; others need fastening gently with special ties or soft string. Even the self-clinging types require a little encouragement to go the right way.

Some flowering climbers will only flower well if the shoots are kept nearly horizontal or bent downwards: if they are allowed to scramble straight up a wall, for instance, flowering may be sparse.

Artificial lighting

If you want to turn winter into a growing season for plants, it's no good just providing warmth: they need light to go with it. Natural daylight can be supplemented by artificial light quite successfully.

Ordinary light bulbs give off too much heat to be useful, but fluorescent light is fine for plants. It needs to be quite close to the plant to do any good: a 40-watt daylight or cool light fluorescent tube should be positioned 45–75 cm (18–30 in) directly

---

·PLANTS TOLERANT OF LOW LIGHT·

Bird's nest fern (*Asplenium nidus*)
Cast iron plant (*Aspidistra elatior*)
Castor oil plant (*Fatsia japonica*)
Chinese evergreen (*Aglaonema crispum* 'Silver Queen', *Aglaonema commutatum*)
Dragon tree (*Dracaena marginata*)
Dumb cane (*Dieffenbachia picta*)
Fiddle-leafed fig (*Ficus lyrata*)
Flamingo plant (*Anthurium scherzerianum*)
Goosefoot plant (*Syngonium podophyllum*)
Grape ivy (*Cissus rhombifolia*)
Ivy (*Hedera helix* – not variegated)
Ivy tree (*Fatshedera lizei*)
Kentia palm (*Howea forsteriana*)
Parlour palm (*Chamaedorea elegans*)
Pineapple plant (*Ananas bracteus*)
Rubber plant (*Ficus elastica*)
Sweetheart vine (*Philodendron scandens*)
Swiss cheese plant (*Monstera deliciosa*)

·HANDY TIP·

When you go on holiday for more than a few days, by far the best plan is to get a neighbour to look after your plants for you. Group them all together in a cool place out of direct sun: the kitchen sink or the bath is often ideal.

above the plants. Fluorescent lights are also available as compact bulbs as well as tubes, which will fit in an ordinary bayonet or Edison screw fitting with an adaptor. These will probably be more suitable for room settings, and easier to set up.

Containers

For the majority of indoor plants, an ordinary plastic plant pot with drainage holes in the base is ideal. They are not particularly attractive, but can be placed inside a decorative pot cover which also helps to protect furniture as it does not have drainage holes.

Some plants grow well in traditional clay (terracotta) pots and large, decorative terracotta planters are ideal for a conservatory. However they are breakable and heavy, and quite expensive. Clay pots dry out more quickly than plastic. They have a single, large drainage hole in the base, whereas plastic pots have a number of slits round the edge. Both types are available in a range of sizes, and in three depths – standard, the shallower half-pot, and the very shallow pan.

Self-watering pots are available. These have a reservoir of water which is fed gradually to the compost. All the grower needs to do is top up the reservoir occasionally. They are useful for situations in which plants are likely to get forgotten (an office, for instance) but not all plants are suitable for growing in them.

Hydroculture

Plants can be grown very successfully under a system known as hydroculture, where they grow in water which contains dissolved nutrients.

A special watertight container is used (Fig. 7), which normally contains an inner mesh pot filled with material to support the plant (usually a light-weight expanded clay aggregate known as Leca) and an outer pot which acts as a reservoir. Water and specially formulated fertilizer is added through a tube marked with a gauge to show exactly when and how much water is needed.

The advantages of this system are its cleanliness and easy maintenance: there is no need to worry about when and how much to water. Plants grown by the hydroculture system are quite expensive, and it has become rather less fashionable than it was when first introduced some 20 or so years ago. It is quite common in maintained displays in public buildings, where it has obvious advantages.

Fig. 7 In this typical hydroculture pot, roots emerge through an inner container filled with Leca granules into an outer container of water and nutrients in solution.

·3·
Using Plants Indoors

Plants can be used to enhance every room within the house, but there are various points to consider when choosing plants for particular areas.

Living rooms

The areas where you spend most of your time are obviously the first places you should think of for displaying plants. After all, it is here you will be able to appreciate them most fully.

Living rooms are generally kept fairly warm in winter, but the temperature can dip suddenly if heating is switched off at night. The atmosphere is usually pretty dry, depending on the type of heating used. There will be some form of artificial lighting for several hours during most of the year, and this could be made to double up as plant lighting. It may also be sufficient to prevent flowering in 'short day' plants such as poinsettias and kalanchoes (these are triggered to begin flowering by decreasing day length). Natural light is usually fairly good, with a reasonable amount of window area.

Choose plants you would be happy to live with. A striking 'architectural' plant may be imposing in an entrance hall but perhaps an uncomfortable companion in a living room.

Kitchen

The kitchen is another place in which a lot of time is spent and where plants are very welcome. The temperature of a kitchen can vary widely depending on how it is used: a large, family kitchen also used as a dining and living room is likely to be kept much warmer than a small, modern 'galley' kitchen used only for preparing and cooking the occasional meal. However the temperature in any kitchen is likely to fluctuate quite widely, rising steeply when cooking is taking place. The atmosphere is often humid and steamy, making it a good place for many plants.

Many kitchens do not have very good light conditions, as window space can be fairly small; kitchens also traditionally tend to be positioned on the north side of the house, where they will be cooler.

Bathroom

Another good place for plants that like a steamy atmosphere is the bathroom (Fig. 8). Light levels vary greatly from one house to another but can be quite good, often coming through obscured glass to give diffuse light which is ideal for those plants that dislike direct sunlight. Like kitchens, bathrooms often face north.

► Living rooms often provide good conditions for plants, with fairly even temperatures and plenty of natural light from large windows. These are rooms where you are likely to spend much of your time, so it is worth making a really good display that you can enjoy.

28

Bathrooms in modern houses tend to be well heated and may be the warmest room in the house. In older houses, they can be cold, with the temperature rising rapidly when someone is taking a bath and falling just as rapidly when they leave. The atmosphere then is both cold and moist, which is a dangerous combination for plants, making them liable to attack by fungal diseases.

Bedroom

In many households, not enough waking hours are spent in the bedroom to greatly appreciate the plants there, and it is one place where plants are often neglected.

Bedrooms tend to be fairly cool, often with an east light through quite a large window area. Choose plants that are not too demanding in their watering requirements, as this may well get forgotten in the morning rush.

Plants with soft, gentle outlines and leaf textures are usually favoured over hard, spiky subjects for bedrooms, though like all other aspects this is very much a matter of personal choice.

Hall

This is the first part of a house a visitor sees; here is where you want to create your first impression.

Whatever their form, plants in a hallway should give a welcoming atmosphere (Fig. 9). If the front door is used only by visitors and not by the family it is important not to forget the plants there: neglected plants can look worse than no plants at all.

A hallway can be a draughty place, so choose tolerant specimens. Not only is there the opening and closing of an outer door to consider, but if stairs are situated in the hall, warm air will tend to rise up them, causing an updraught. The hall is usually cooler than living areas, but the temperature tends to be even, without wide fluctuations.

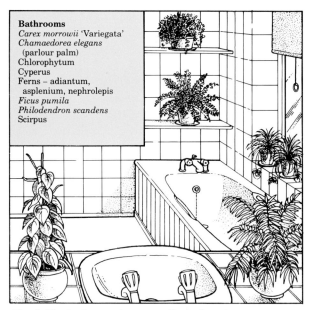

Bathrooms
Carex morrowii 'Variegata'
Chamaedorea elegans
  (parlour palm)
Chlorophytum
Cyperus
Ferns – adiantum,
  asplenium, nephrolepis
Ficus pumila
Philodendron scandens
Scirpus

Fig. 8 The bathroom is an excellent place to grow moisture-loving plants that will revel in the steamy atmosphere.

Halls and cool rooms
Aglaonema commutatum
Aspidistra elatior
Chlorophytum comosum
Cissus antarctica
Hedera helix
Primula obconica
Tradescantia fluminensis

Fig. 9 Create a welcoming atmosphere in your hallway with plants tolerant of draughts, and sometimes low light levels.

Garden room

A garden room or conservatory is usually a place designed with plants in mind, but that also has to double up as a living area. Designs of these rooms vary greatly, but they normally all have good light.

The type of plants you grow in a garden room will depend entirely on the way in which it is used and furnished, and whether plants or people are the most important. We take a detailed look at garden rooms and conservatories in the next chapter.

POSITIONING PLANTS

Positioning a plant within a room is not simply a matter of putting it where it looks best. There are several other points that have to be considered (Fig. 10).

Possibly the most important is whether the light conditions are right. The darkest areas in a room are, perhaps surprisingly, either side of a window. The brightest area is directly in front of a window, with the light falling off quite rapidly as you move further back (see again Fig. 5 on p. 19).

The furnishings within a room also play a large part in its overall brightness. Light colours reflect most light, and light-coloured walls and carpets will make a great deal of difference to the light available to plants. Dull areas can be lightened by the use of light wall colours, carefully placed mirrors, and artificial lighting.

If a plant is placed near a one-sided light source, it will tend to lean towards the light, and its leaves will all face that way. Giving the plant a quarter-turn each day will prevent this (Fig. 4 on p. 19).

Windowsills are obvious places to put plants but they may not be ideal. The light levels will be high, but sunlight falling through the glass can scorch foliage. If you regularly draw the curtains, foliage can be damaged by being regularly bruised; the same goes for plants positioned too near throughways, where people are constantly brushing past (Fig. 10).

An area near a frequently used door is going to be draughty, and is not the best place for plants. Hot spots should be avoided, too: not just the obvious

| Wall plants dry out quickly. Do not place them where the furnishings below may be damaged by drips | Foliage too close to chairs is likely to be damaged when the chair is used | Watch out for 'hot spots' over electrical equipment and radiators | Spreading plants on windowsills may be damaged when the curtains are drawn |

Fig. 10 Care must be taken when positioning plants within a room, as problems may result from a variety of causes.

▲ Plants can be grouped
very successfully in a range
of containers. Make sure all
the subjects chosen like
similar growing conditions.

► A landing can be a
difficult place for plants,
but here full use has been
made of the available light,
creating a most effective
display.

ones over radiators, but above television sets, cookers and refrigerators, too. Plants in hanging pots are very attractive, but remember that they will drip when watered; make sure there is nothing underneath that can be damaged.

Watering needs to be done frequently, so make the task easy. If the position of a plant means it's a struggle to water it, you are both going to suffer.

Do protect valuable furniture and furnishings. Provide each pot with a suitable saucer to catch the overflow from watering, and take care when misting plant foliage – it is surprising what a large area the droplets cover. Check plants frequently for pests, as sticky honeydew from an aphid infestation can ruin fabrics and wooden surfaces. Occasional overwatering of a plant at floor level soon leads to spoiled, mouldy carpets. Bear all these things in mind when deciding on the best position for plants.

Most plants and plant groups look best displayed against a plain background, particularly finely cut or strongly variegated foliage. Patterned wallpaper demands bold foliage and strong plant shapes. The use of spotlights can create dramatic effects as shadows are cast against the wall or ceiling, or the plant is thrown into silhouette.

Grouping plants

Displaying plants in groups is not only attractive, it provides good growing conditions for the plants, as a humid microclimate is formed within the group.

There are several ways in which to display plants in groups. The simplest is just to bring a collection of plants in their individual pots together on a table or windowsill: alternatively the plants may be arranged within another container. They may either remain within their individual pots or be planted directly into the larger container (Fig. 11).

Planting in a single container has certain drawbacks. First, the plants must all like similar compost and watering regimes, and secondly the roots soon grow together to make the group inseparable. If you want to give the appearance of a group growing together, it is often best to keep the plants in their own pots, sinking them into peat, sphagnum moss, gravel or a similar material to hide the pots. Then their individual watering needs can be attended to, and a plant which is not thriving can be removed and replaced.

The plants chosen to make up the group should like similar conditions of light, humidity and temperature. You may like to arrange a group of plants of similar type and appearance or markedly contrasting styles.

Containers for groups

A variety of suitable containers are available in garden centres, made of wood, pottery, brass or plastic, in lots of different shapes or designs. Plants can also be grouped very successfully in household items such as plastic bowls, wicker shopping baskets, waste-paper bins, wooden boxes, and a wide variety of others. Those that are not waterproof should be lined with plastic before use.

Fig. 11 Plants grow well grouped together, but it is a good idea to keep them in their individual pots, surrounded by moist peat on a layer of pea gravel or similar material.

Pea gravel

33

BOTTLE GARDENS AND TERRARIA

Plants which enjoy a humid atmosphere can be grown in an enclosed bottle garden or terrarium very successfully. They make their own mini world, and can survive for a long time without any maintenance or interference from us.

The normal container which is used is a glass carboy. Those which are specially made for using as bottle gardens have a wide opening at the top to make planting up easier, but unfortunately they are often tinted deep green, which means plants will not thrive in them. Clear or very lightly tinted ones are more suitable. Other glass containers can also be used for plants: goldfish bowls covered with self-clinging plastic film, sweet jars, large storage jars, and even tightly covered brandy glasses can be successful.

Terraria are attractive glass cases like miniature greenhouses, in varying shapes and sizes. They can be highly decorative but very expensive. Plastic types are not so attractive but a lot cheaper: unfortunately most of these are heavily tinted too. They are much easier to plant up than a bottle garden (see Fig. 27 on p. 74).

1. The bottle or terrarium should be washed and thoroughly dried before it is planted up. For a carboy with a small opening, you will need a piece of stiff paper rolled to form a funnel, and long-handled planting tools – usually a dessert spoon and fork lashed to canes.

2. In the base of the bottle (using the paper funnel) or terrarium, place a layer of gravel for drainage up to 5 cm (2 in) deep. Adjust the depth to suit the size of the container.

3. Next sprinkle a layer of charcoal, then a 5–8 cm (2–3 in) layer of peat-based (or peat-substitute) compost. This can be 'landscaped' with a slight slope for extra interest.

4. Plan the arrangement of plants before putting them in the container, taking into account whether the bottle garden is to be viewed from one side or all round. Remove all dead and dying leaves and flowers from the plants. Take them out of their pots and tease out or trim the rootball if necessary. Set them in the compost and firm lightly. Once planted up, the surface of the compost can be covered with a thin layer of fine grit.

5. Trickle a little water down the sides of the bottle to clean the glass and just moisten the compost. Stop up the opening of the bottle garden or close the door of the terrarium and place in a well-lit location, but out of direct sun. The inside of the glass will mist over to start with; if this does not clear of its own accord the lid can be removed for a short while. Once the plants settle down the garden is likely to mist over each morning but clear by itself after a short while. If the unit is kept sealed it is unlikely to need watering for a considerable time.

Suitable plants include earth star (cryptanthus), snakeskin plant (fittonia), creeping fig (*Ficus pumila*), club mosses (selaginella) and small ferns.

·EASY-TO-GROW PLANTS·

Angels' tears (*Billbergia nutans*)
Aspidistra (*Aspidistra elatior*)
Busy Lizzie (*Impatiens walleriana*)
Flaming Katy (*Kalanchoe blossfeldiana*)
Grape ivy (*Cissus rhombifolia*)
Ivy (*Hedera varieties*)
Jade plant (*Crassula argentea*)
Kaffir lily (*Clivia miniata*)
Mother-in-law's tongue (*Sansevieria trifasciata*)
Piggy-back plant (*Tolmiea menziesii*)
Lemon-scented pelargonium (*Pelargonium crispum*)
Umbrella plant (*Cyperus alternifolius*)
Wandering Jew (*Tradescantia fluminensis*)

Avoid very rapid-growing plants which will swamp the others, and flowering plants. Dead flowers cannot easily be removed and will soon rot, generally leading to the rest of the plants succumbing to fungus diseases.

CLIMBERS AND TRAILERS

Climbing plants generally need training up some form of support to keep them shapely and attractive. They may attach themselves to suitable surfaces by aerial roots, like scindapsus and Swiss cheese plant; they may hang on with tightly curling tendrils, like the passion flower; or the stems may simply twine round their support, like jasmine.

A moss pole is ideal for plants with aerial roots. This can be made from a cylinder of chicken wire stuffed with sphagnum moss, or moss bound tightly round a stake. Synthetic substitutes have also been used satisfactorily. Make sure the pole is set securely in the pot. The moss is kept moist, and aerial roots soon take hold, though the shoots will need tying into place to start with.

Other forms of support which can be set in the pot include wooden, wire or plastic trellis or hoops, or three or four thin canes wound round with wire. A more permanent arrangement is to fix a trellis to a wall and allow the plant to climb up that: use battens to hold the trelliswork clear of the wall and enable it to be taken down for cleaning and decorating. Free-standing trellis covered with climbing plants can make an attractive room divider.

Fix shoots gently to their supports with plant ties or soft twine in a figure-of-eight. Never tie stems tightly. When shoots reach the tops of their supports they can be trained back down or pinched out as desired. Flowering climbers should have the shoots trained horizontally or bent downwards at some point to slow the flow of sap and encourage flower buds.

Trailing plants have stems which cascade downwards; many climbers will trail satisfactorily if their shoots are not supported (Fig. 12). Obviously the plants must be set in a position where the stems can trail satisfactorily: on a pedestal, a table or window-sill, or in a hanging pot. Many trailers need regular pinching out of the young shoots to prevent the plant becoming straggly.

Fig. 12 An attractive feature can be made by building up a tiered display of suitable plants in pots of decreasing size.

◀ Climbing house plants such as ivy can be trained up a trellis – or simply allowed to trail gracefully.

▶ Large plant displays in the reception areas of offices and public buildings are often set up and cared for by specialist contractors.

OFFICES AND WORKPLACES

Plants give any workplace a more congenial atmosphere, but conditions are often far from ideal. Unless one or two people are given the specific task of looking after the plants, they are likely to end up either neglected or suffering from over-attention. Plants provided by the company are often disregarded, but those bought by employees for their own desks are far more likely to be well cared for.

Workplaces are often deprived of natural light, and suffer from temperature fluctuations when the heating is switched off outside working hours. Plants are left to fend for themselves at weekends and for longer breaks, when unexpected sunshine or cold weather can cause havoc. Plant pots are a traditional receptacle for cigarette ends and the dregs from coffee cups. Fumes from various industrial processes and even typewriter correction fluid can cause problems, though plants have actually been found to improve the atmosphere for workers by removing pollutants from the air.

Plants may be banned from certain areas on safety grounds, and when watering plants it must be remembered that wet floors can be particularly hazardous in workplaces.

One place where plants are normally welcomed is in the reception area of a business, where they

create a welcoming atmosphere for customers and can make a statement about the prosperity and style of the company. Large displays may be set up, which are cared for by a team of specialist contractors, or smaller groups can be cared for by the staff. Specimen plants are particularly useful in these areas.

When selecting plants for a workplace, it is therefore obvious that tolerant specimens are most likely to survive. Favourites include the familiar spider plant (chlorophytum) and Wandering Jew (zebrina): though they may most frequently be seen struggling in discarded plastic coffee cups, there is no reason why they should not be given attractive

pots or hanging baskets and allowed to make a good display. Mother-in-law's-tongue will put up with a good deal of ill treatment and given a chance will make a fine specimen. Rubber plants, ivies and Swiss cheese plants will also survive less than ideal conditions and will amply reward a little encouragement.

Give workplace plants the lightest positions available, and use self-watering pots or hydro-culture systems if these will help make them easy to care for. Give responsibility for their care to one enthusiastic employee – but don't hold them wholly responsible for other workers' mistreatment of the plants!

Conservatories and Garden Rooms

The Victorian conservatory was devoted to plants; it was very much a growing area, raising plants to be displayed in the house as they reached perfection. It may have been attached to the house or completely separate, and was usually heated by a boiler and a system of hot water pipes.

Conservatories were a feature of large houses and wealthy families that could afford to employ a team of gardeners. After the Victorian era, conservatories became rare; many of those that were in existence fell into disrepair or found other uses. In recent years, conservatories have once again become popular, though on a completely different scale to those grand Victorian edifices.

Modern conservatories come in a wide range of sizes, styles and materials. They need not be expensive, and are frequently used as a cheap way of providing a home extension. While plants still have priority in some, most must double up to provide extra living space for the family, while some are quite simply sun rooms, without a plant in sight! For those who love plants, a conservatory will be filled with greenery and flowers while still providing a pleasant place to eat or simply relax and enjoy the surroundings. You must decide whether people or plants will have priority before you choose and plan a new conservatory, as this will affect some important and basic decisions.

How you intend to use your conservatory will also determine how you furnish it. There's no point laying expensive carpet in a room that is going to be filled with plants, watering cans and compost!

The line between conservatories and sun rooms or garden rooms is rather indistinct. A conservatory in which plants are going to be an important feature should generally be constructed very largely of glass or similar transparent material. It may have glass to ground level, or perhaps half walls of brick or stone or even timber, but it should have a translucent roof for maximum light transmission. If you don't have the luxury of a conservatory, however, almost any well-lit room can be turned into a garden room where plants predominate.

Choosing a conservatory

Most conservatories will be a fairly substantial investment, so it is worth taking time over choosing one that will suit your needs. Money will probably be a limiting factor for most households, so the first thing to do is set your price limit, then decide on the size and style that you can afford.

Browse round a few garden building centres to get an idea of the sort of thing that is available, and get hold of as many brochures as possible. Decide on a style that will complement your house (Fig. 13): an ultra-modern design on a period home will not usually sit comfortably, nor will an ornate, Victorian-style conservatory tacked on to a brand new estate house.

Plastic-glazed conservatories are available, but glass is the choice for most people. The roof of a conservatory, however, is usually plastic (twin wall polycarbonate is a favourite material) for safety reasons, though it may be reinforced glass. All glazing should be done with toughened safety glass; if you have young children, consider whether solid lower walls might be a better option. Double glazing increases the cost but cuts down slightly on winter heating bills and keeps out noise.

The structure may be timber, metal or uPVC.

• *Timber* is a traditional material and may be first choice for a conservatory for an older style house; it needs more maintenance than either of the other two materials. Western red cedar has the most resistance to decay: pressure-treated softwoods are also available.

• *Metal frames* – usually aluminium – have a choice of plain, bronzed or white finishes and are virtually maintenance free. They are generally used for modern-style conservatories.

• *uPVC* is also maintenance free, and is often used as the frame for sun rooms at the cheaper end of the market (Fig. 14). On a high quality model it can look just as good as white-painted timber.

Don't forget to equip your conservatory with adequate ventilators. While extra vents can sometimes be added later, this is not always possible. A combination of roof and side vents gives the best airflow; vital for both people and plants in sunny weather. Extra vents to the standard design can often be specified at the initial ordering stage, and other accessories, such as blinds, furniture and flooring, may also be available.

Siting

The siting of the conservatory calls for careful consideration. A south-east or south-west facing

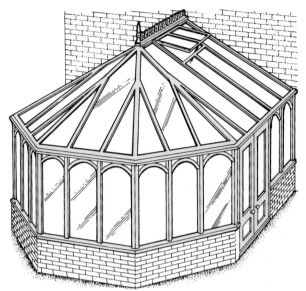

Fig. 13 Choose a style of conservatory that blends with your house. This traditional, Victorian style would suit an older building.

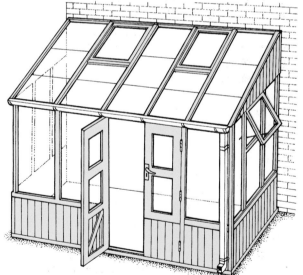

Fig. 14 The sun room is more basic and less luxurious than a conservatory, but its high proportion of glass still makes it a good place for plants.

aspect is usually better than north, which gets too little sun, or south, which gets too much, making the conservatory unbearably hot in summer. If you would like to breakfast in your conservatory you will probably want it to face east. If you will spend most time there when you come home from work in the evening, west would most likely be your choice.

But of course, it might not be possible or practical to build on to these aspects of the house, and there are other points to consider, too. Which existing room will the conservatory adjoin? The living room is probably first choice, but perhaps the kitchen would be a more practical proposition? What about water and electricity supply, and existing drains and cables? These points need to be discussed with a builder before a decision is made.

Planning permission is not necessarily required, but in certain circumstances it will be. The only safe way is to check with your local authority at an early stage, giving an idea of size, style and position of the proposed conservatory. They will advise whether a formal application needs to be made.

Flooring

The type of floor you choose will soon tell whether you are a real plant lover or whether you want a conservatory simply as extra living space!

Where there are plants, there are likely to be water spills. If you are a keen plant grower, you will want to provide a humid atmosphere in your conservatory: good for the plants, but not so good for floor coverings and furnishings. If the conservatory is to be the true link between house and garden that many people hope, muddy footprints are likely to be a frequent feature. And unless you are lucky enough to have a separate greenhouse in which to do all your potting, pruning and propagating, compost and plant debris will inevitably end up on the floor, no matter how tidy you try to be.

The best type of floor, therefore, is one that can cope with all this–a solid, waterproof surface that can be brushed down and wiped over. At the same time, if the conservatory is going to be used for people to relax in, the floor needs to be moderately attractive and comfortable to live with. Ceramic tiles provide one of the best answers: they are hard wearing but attractive, giving a light, airy, 'Continental' atmosphere. Available in a wide range of colours and patterns, they can be quite expensive. Make sure they have a non-slip surface.

Somewhat cheaper but still attractive are some of the many styles of garden paving available. Those that have the appearance of riven stone look particularly good, but can be rough and uneven: a polished marble type of surface may be better. Vinyl flooring is a possibility, but beware water seeping underneath, causing it to lift: wood block flooring poses similar problems. These surfaces are acceptable if only the occasional water spill, quickly cleaned up, is likely to take place.

Carpets make the conservatory a pleasant living area, but are not the most practical choice. However, kitchen carpeting, which is resistant to stains and spills, could be suitable, and carpet tiles allow replacement of small areas which become badly soiled. Carpeting a smallish area adjoining the house, while choosing a more practical flooring for the rest of the conservatory, is a good compromise. Carpets also have the advantage of making the conservatory a much warmer and more comfortable place in the winter. If loose rugs are used for winter they can be taken out during the summer – but rugs can be dangerous on a polished surface.

You may wish to have a permanent bed for plants in one part of the conservatory, and in this case, one

▶ Plants still have priority in some conservatories, though most must now double up to provide attractive extra living space for the family as well as plants.

Fig. 15 Built-in beds on the conservatory floor are a very satisfactory way of growing plants, preventing the problem of compost drying out.

area could be left as bare soil (Fig. 15), but most gardeners choose to grow all their plants in containers.

Whatever type of flooring you eventually decide on, ensure that the concrete base for it is level and completely dry before installation.

Furnishings

Like the flooring, furnishings need to be adapted to the sort of use the conservatory is going to get. Cane furniture has a traditional, colonial style, but won't put up with too much water being splashed about. Any non-painted wooden furniture is likely to suffer in a very damp, humid atmosphere. The more comfortable types of garden furniture are very useful, as they are made of water-resisting plastic or tubular steel, and have soft covers and cushions that can easily be removed as necessary.

If your conservatory is definitely a place where plants come first, the same type of slatted staging that is used in greenhouses will be useful to place pots and trays on.

Heating

Having invested in a conservatory, most people will want to use it all year round. This means heating in the winter, and probably for at least part of the autumn and spring. When the sun is shining, a surprising amount of heat will be trapped by the glass even when it is very cold outside, but on dull winter days, particularly if the floor is solid, an unheated conservatory can be a very chilly place.

If possible, arrange for the house heating system to be extended to the conservatory when it is being built, but ensure that the conservatory has its own controls, as its heat requirements may be very

· WINTER-FLOWERING PLANTS ·	
Name	**Description**
Azalea	Flowers in shades of red, white and pink; needs acid soil
Begonia	Several varieties flower in winter, including the popular Rieger begonias; single or double, in red, pink, yellow and orange
Bulbs	A wide range of bulbs can be forced for a winter display
Cineraria	Daisy-like flowers in shades of pink, red, blue and white
Cyclamen	Both large and miniature varieties are available, flowering for much of the winter
Hippeastrum	Popular large bulbs with flamboyant, trumpet-shaped flowers
Jasmine	White, starry scented flowers; vigorous twiner
Kalanchoe	Long-lasting flowerheads on a succulent-leaved plant
Poinsettia	A Christmas favourite. Brilliant red bracts; also pink, white and variegated varieties
Primula	Several different species and varieties with colourful flowers in a wide range of colours

different from the rest of the house. If it is not possible to extend the existing heating, a number of options are open to you.

• *Paraffin heaters* tend to be messy, smelly and inconvenient, and burning paraffin produces large quantities of water vapour. These heaters are more suitable for greenhouses than living areas.

• *Calor gas* is a possibility. These heaters again produce water vapour as a by-product.

• *Electricity* is generally the cleanest and most convenient method of supplementary heating. Thermostatically controlled fan heaters can be set to the required temperature and will switch themselves on and off as necessary, but they can be intrusively noisy.

In fact, almost any type of room heater can be used in a conservatory, but a balance must be drawn between very humid air which could damage fittings and furnishings, and very dry air which is not good for plants.

Shading and ventilation

You may want to take advantage of every scrap of sunshine there is in the winter, but come summer and you will soon find it becomes uncomfortably hot. Some form of shading is essential to protect the plants as well as to make it a more pleasant environment for people.

The cheapest form of shading is a paint-on 'whitewash' that can be fairly easily removed with a dry duster at the end of the season. While this is perfectly adequate for greenhouses, it does not look very attractive on a conservatory. Green or black netting can be fixed in place on the outside of the conservatory, or thin white netting will give a light sunscreen when attached to the inside.

Blinds are the best type of shading, however. They can be external or internal, and operated with guide cords and pulleys for easy raising and lowering according to the weather conditions. They are most easily fitted right from the start, when the conservatory is being constructed.

If you are out of the house for most of the day, you will need to remember to lower the blinds before you leave in the summer, even on dull days. If it brightens up later, irreparable damage could be done to tender-leaved plants. You will also find it very useful to fit some form of automatic vent-

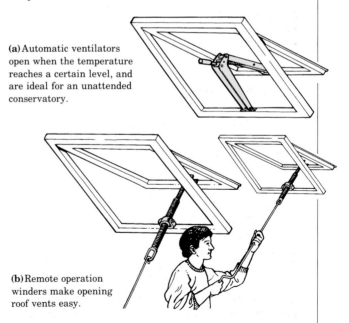

(a) Automatic ventilators open when the temperature reaches a certain level, and are ideal for an unattended conservatory.

(b) Remote operation winders make opening roof vents easy.

Fig. 16 Adequate ventilation is very important for a conservatory. Various types of vent are available.

·CLIMBERS FOR CONSERVATORIES·

Name	Description
Bougainvillea glabra	A scrambling climber with glossy oval leaves and colourful bracts in shades of purple, rose and red
Cup-and-saucer vine (*Cobaea scandens*)	Large, open-trumpet shaped flowers that start off cream and turn rich purple; fast-growing stems with tendrils; quite easy to raise from seed and treat as annual
Gloriosa (*Gloriosa superba*)	Long, thin tubers produce stems which cling by tendrils; flowers are red and yellow, with reflexed petals having wavy edges; long stamens
Lobster claw, parrot's bill (*Clianthus puniceus*)	Woody scrambler with fresh green leaves of ferny leaflets. Curiously shaped, bright red flowers in spring and summer
Mandevilla splendens	A twiner with glossy green leaves and beautiful rose-pink, yellow centred, trumpet-shaped flowers
Passion flower (*Passiflora caerulea, P. coccinea, P. quadrangularis*)	Palmate leaves and spectacular flowers in summer – *P. caerulea* is blue and white, *P. coccinea* a glowing crimson and *P. quadrangularis* red, white and violet; all fast growing
Wax plant (*Hoya carnosa*)	Fleshy leaves on long, twining stems; bunches of pendulous, waxy white flowers with red centres

openers so that the vents can be opened as the temperature rises (Fig. 16). Again, if you are likely to be out of the house a lot, you will need to bear security in mind. Louvred ventilators at the base of the conservatory and the main vents in the roof will be most secure; and don't forget to lock the doors from the conservatory into the house.

◀ **Effective shading and good ventilation are both essential to prevent over-heating in a conservatory.**

▶ **A sun room can be a good place for an informal plant display, especially if shelves are fitted.**

·5·
Propagation

A cheap way to increase your stock of indoor plants is to raise new ones yourself, from seed, cuttings or division. Not all plants can be raised successfully at home, but many can. They make take a few years to reach a reasonable size or may give you a mature plant in one season. However long the wait, there is a great deal of satisfaction in propagating a plant yourself.

Most propagation is undertaken in spring and early summer. A greenhouse provides excellent conditions for many types of propagation. Thermostatically controlled heating provides a constant temperature and good light conditions enable young plants to grow sturdily. Some form of shading is usually necessary to keep direct sunlight off very young plants, however. The greenhouse should be equipped with staging (benching) to raise the plants to working height: slatted staging is best, as water does not collect as it would on a solid surface.

Usually only a part of the greenhouse is required for propagating purposes, and for raising cuttings a purpose-built propagating bench is ideal. This usually consists of a boxed-in section half filled with sand, through which a soil heating cable runs to provide heat at the base of the cuttings, where it is needed. The sand is topped with sowing compost in which the cuttings are inserted. The top and sides of the unit are covered with a polythene tent, and a mist unit senses the amount of water in the atmosphere, supplying a very fine mist of water over the top of the cuttings whenever it is necessary.

For those who require rather less sophisticated (and less expensive) equipment, a heated propagator is a good buy. This again provides warmth through a soil heating cable, and humidity is kept high by a plastic cover. Heated propagators are available in a wide range of sizes and prices. Unheated propagators are simply trays with a well-fitting, ventilated clear plastic lid.

But none of this equipment is actually necessary, though it will certainly speed up propagation and help prevent failures. Some shallow trays and pots, plastic pot covers or polythene bags, and some seed and cuttings compost, either loam based or soil-less, plus a warm, bright place, are all that are required.

CUTTINGS

This is the method by which the majority of indoor plants are raised. A cutting is a portion of plant which is encouraged to develop roots, or shoots, or sometimes both, and become a complete new plant. There are two types – stem and leaf cuttings.

Stem cuttings (Fig. 17)
Indoor plants are propagated from soft stem cuttings, using young, strongly growing shoots.

1. Select a healthy young shoot, preferably without flower buds, and remove it from the parent plant. Use a sharp, clean knife or razor blade to cut it cleanly just above a leaf joint, taking care not to leave a long snag on the parent which could die back.

2. Trim the shoot immediately below a leaf joint and remove the lower leaves. The size of the cutting will depend upon the type of plant you are propagating, but it should generally have one large or two small fully opened leaves at the top, and two to four leaves removed from the base to allow the stem to be inserted in the compost.

3. Dip the base of the cutting into a small amount of hormone rooting powder plus fungicide to speed rooting and help prevent rotting. Tap the stem to make sure that only a light dusting of powder remains; too much will have an adverse effect. Rooting powder is not essential; many cuttings root well without it.

4. Fill a pot or tray right to the top with seed and cuttings compost and firm it down lightly with the base of another pot or a flat wooden presser. Topping it with a thin layer of sharp sand helps prevent cuttings from rotting.

5. Make a hole in the compost with a pencil or dibber and insert the cutting, making sure the base is in firm contact with the compost. Firm it in lightly with your fingers. Space further cuttings so that the leaves do not touch.

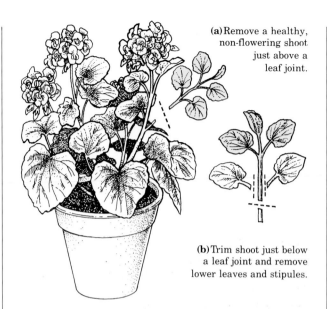

(a) Remove a healthy, non-flowering shoot just above a leaf joint.

(b) Trim shoot just below a leaf joint and remove lower leaves and stipules.

Fig. 17 Soft stem cutting of pelargonium.

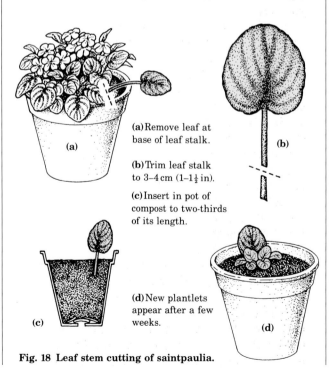

(a) Remove leaf at base of leaf stalk.

(b) Trim leaf stalk to 3–4 cm (1–1½ in).

(c) Insert in pot of compost to two-thirds of its length.

(d) New plantlets appear after a few weeks.

Fig. 18 Leaf stem cutting of saintpaulia.

6. Water the completed pot using a fine rose on the watering can, cover with a clear plastic top (or with a plastic bag held clear of the cuttings by short canes) and place in a warm – about 20°C (68°F) – bright position out of direct sun.

Keep the compost just moist and remove the plastic cover if there is a great deal of condensation (the aim is to keep the atmosphere humid but not saturated). Within a fairly short time, roots will start to form at the base of the stems. You can tell when this has happened because the centres of the plants start to look 'growy' and fresh; a very gentle tug at a cutting will give slight resistance, and eventually roots can be seen at the drainage holes of the container. Always leave the cuttings until you are sure they have rooted before testing them or you could easily tear off the newly forming roots.

Leaf cuttings (Fig. 18)
Some plants will also produce roots and shoots from leaf veins or leaf stems. Saintpaulias, or African violets, are easy to raise from leaf stems.

1. Remove a fully opened, healthy leaf by cutting with a sharp knife or razor right at the base of the leaf stalk. Handle the leaf very carefully, as it will bruise easily.

2. Trim the base of the leaf stalk so that it is 3–4 cm (1–1½ in) long. Dip into hormone rooting powder and insert at the edge of a small pot filled with seed and cuttings compost as for stem cuttings. About two-thirds of the leaf stem should be buried. Firm in gently but thoroughly.

3. Water the compost so that it is just moist and place the pot in a lightly shaded, warm position. There is no need to cover the pot.

Within about eight weeks, new plantlets will be pushing up through the soil at the base of the leaf.

Keep the compost just moist until the pot is nearly filled with foliage, then turn the cluster of plantlets carefully out of the pot, tease them into separate plants and pot them up individually.

Plants can also be raised from the leaf veins of some species (Fig. 19). Cape primrose (strepto-carpus) will provide several plants from one of its long leaves. Choose a healthy leaf, as usual, and remove it cleanly from the parent. Cut the leaf across into three or four sections with a very sharp knife or razor blade and dust a little rooting powder on to the lower cut surface of each section. Insert the sections to about a third of their depth in a pot or tray of compost and water lightly as for leaf stem cuttings. They will produce plantlets in the same way.

DIVISION

Plants that grow in clumps rather than as single stems can often be propagated simply by dividing the clump into smaller pieces. Plants are usually left until they have filled their container before they are split in this way.

Turn the plant out of its pot and carefully remove some of the compost until you can see where the sections are joined together. Plantlets can then be separated at this point, either by teasing them gently apart or by cutting through with a sharp knife. The separate portions can then be potted up in suitable size containers of potting compost. Keep them out of direct sun for a while and take care not to overwater them.

Plants that can be divided include Mother-in-law's-tongue (sansevieria), cyperus, maidenhair fern and many other ferns, syngonium and plenty of others.

Some plants produce smaller plantlets round their edge, and these are known as offsets. Many succulents like echeveria and sempervivum do this;

▲ Clump-forming plants, e.g. saintpaulia, are divisible. Take care not to damage the crowns.

▶ Spider plants are very easy to propagate, forming dozens of baby plantlets.

angel's tears or billbergia is another. These offsets can usually be removed without disturbing the parent plant too much. Again, they may need cutting off with a sharp knife. They may already be rooted, or may form roots quickly when potted up individually.

LAYERING

A layer is rather like a cutting that is not removed from the parent plant, but left attached. It has the benefit of receiving nutrients and water from the rest of the plant while it is growing its own roots. It is only separated from the parent when it is already rooted and capable of leading a separate existence.

Plants with trailing stems, such as ivies, can be layered by pegging a young, healthy shoot into a pot of seed and cuttings compost. If the stem is

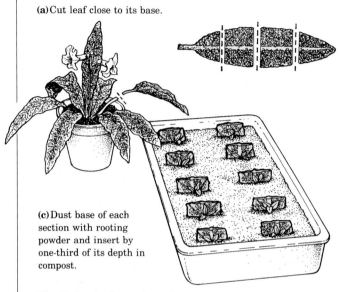

(a) Cut leaf close to its base.

(c) Dust base of each section with rooting powder and insert by one-third of its depth in compost.

Fig. 19 Leaf vein cutting of streptocarpus.

1. Make a sloping cut about one-third of the way through the stem with a sharp knife, just below the lowest leaves. Dust it with rooting powder and wedge it open with a matchstick or small wad of sphagnum moss.

2. Pack round the wounded area with moist sphagnum moss, then wrap a piece of clear polythene round the whole thing and tape the top and bottom firmly to hold it in place. If you cannot get sphagnum moss, you can use peat instead, but it is a little more tricky: you will need to attach the polythene sleeve first, then fill it up with moist peat.

3. Care for the plant in the normal way. After some time, fine roots will become visible within the moss, and when the layer is well rooted it can be cut off with sharp secateurs, the polythene unwrapped, and the rooted layer potted up.

woody, it is usual to wound it by scraping off a piece of bark from the underside near a leaf node, or cutting a small slit part way through the stem. This encourages roots to form at that point.

Secure it into the compost with a piece of wire bent into a hairpin, or weigh it down with a pebble, and keep the compost just moist until roots form.

Some plants, like the spider plant (chlorophytum) are so keen to propagate themselves in this way that they form dozens of small plantlets on the ends of long runners. They may form roots even before they touch the compost!

Air layering (Fig. 20)
This is a little different. If a stem cannot easily be brought to a pot of compost, it is left where it is and the 'compost' is brought to it. Rubber plants are frequently propagated in this way, and the time to do this is when it has become lanky, with bare lower stems.

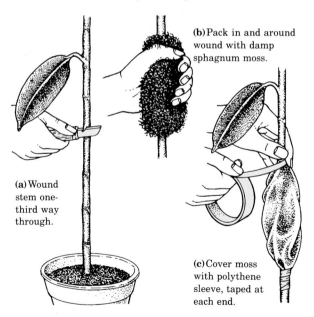

(b) Pack in and around wound with damp sphagnum moss.

(a) Wound stem one-third way through.

(c) Cover moss with polythene sleeve, taped at each end.

Fig. 20 Air layering a rubber plant.

4. The remaining stump need not be discarded: it can be cut down to about 23 cm (9 in) and will often throw out new shoots and become a bushy new plant.

Leaf embryos

Some plants make themselves very easy to propagate by naturally producing complete, tiny plantlets on their leaves. These can be detached from the mother plant and grown on with very little difficulty.

One of the most notable plants that performs this feat is the Mexican hat plant, *Bryophyllum daigremontianum*, and its relation, *Bryophyllum pinnata*. Plantlets crowd round the edges or at the tips of the leaves, each with a pair of leaflets and tiny, thread-like roots. When the mother plant is disturbed, these baby plantlets drop off and quickly take root on the surface of the compost. They can be removed from here and potted up, or they can be lifted from the mother plant before they fall and grow on.

The pig-a-back plant, *Tolmiea menziesii*, produces young plants at the base of the leaf, where it joins the leaf stalk. These make quite an attractive feature when left in position, but if you require to increase the plant, whole leaves can be removed complete with their cargo of baby plants, and should be laid flat on the surface of a tray or pot of moist seed and cuttings compost. Ensure the base of the leaf is in good contact with the compost, and keep the leaves in a humid atmosphere by covering the tray with a propagator top, and misting regularly with a hand sprayer. The young plants will soon develop their own roots and begin to grow away.

The fern *Asplenium bulbiferum* also produces leaf embryos over its pinnate leaves: the leaves should be treated like those of the pig-a-back plant for propagation purposes.

SEED

Several indoor plants can be raised successfully from seed, though for some it will be several years before they reach a reasonable size. One of the main benefits of seed is that it is a very cheap way to obtain plants, and it is particularly useful if a large number of plants are required for a display.

Most of the specially selected varieties with special features such as variegation, compact habit, flower colour and so on, will not breed true from seed. The characteristics they have been selected for have been perpetuated by taking cuttings or other methods of vegetative propagation, and these characteristics are not normally carried through the seed. Seedling from these plants will usually have reverted to the original species.

Some plant varieties which are raised from seed will be F1 hybrids. This means that a breeding programme has been carried out, and two different varieties have been crossed to produce the hybrid (F1 means first generation). These plants often have 'hybrid vigour' – they grow more strongly than either of the parents. Due to the laws of genetics, however, seed saved from one of the hybrids will produce a mixed batch of plants: some of each of the original parent plants, plus some of the hybrids. So it is not worth saving your own seed from F1 hybrid varieties.

Some types of indoor plant are very difficult to raise from seed. The seed may not be freely available, and it may require very specialized,

◄ Many indoor plants are quite simple to raise from soft tip cuttings. Late spring and early summer are usually the most successful times to take them.

► Ferns do not produce seeds; instead they produce large numbers of spores on the undersides of their leaves.

controlled conditions of warmth and moisture before it will germinate. Other plants, however, are quite easy – coleus, for instance, is very simple to grow, will produce useful-sized plants in one season, and is readily available from all the major seed companies.

Choose the easy types unless you can provide the conditions required for both germination and growing on (the seedlings are also likely to need specialized conditions for some time). Among easy and readily available seeds are begonias, coleus, fuchsias, cyclamen, primulas, silk oak (grevillea), and the sensitive plant, *Mimosa pudica*.

Pelargoniums are also freely available, though the hybrid types are quite expensive. Cactus seed is not difficult, and of course some attractive house plants can be raised from fruit pips. Citrus of all types germinate and grow quickly. Avocados are popular with children, who enjoy watching the large stone split and the seed leaves emerge, and many of the exotic fruits now available in supermarkets will produce pleasing and interesting foliage plants.

Equipment
Sowing does not require much specialized equipment. A good brand of seed compost is

necessary, and this is normally peat or peat-substitute based compost, but the loam-based John Innes types are useful for some plants, such as cacti. A range of pots and seed trays can be used. Normally only a small amount of seed will be sown so use half trays rather than full size ones.

For many house plants a propagator will be very useful. Quite high soil temperatures are often required for germination, and a heated propagator will provide this. The covers also help provide the humid atmosphere that is necessary. However, seed can be germinated in a warm place in the home (the airing cupboard is often a good choice). Cover the pots or trays with plastic covers or polythene bags to prevent drying out. It is more difficult to regulate the temperature in an airing cupboard or similar place than in a thermostatically controlled propagator, of course, so you may not be successful with the more demanding species, but many plants can be raised without any specialized equipment.

Sowing seeds (Fig. 21)
1. Fill the container with compost, pushing it well into the corners of a seed tray. Heap it up in the tray and strike it off level with a straight edge. Use a piece of wood cut to the same size as the tray or pot for a presser, to lightly firm and level the compost (or you can use another tray or pot of the same size for this job).

2. Stand the tray or pot in water for about 30 minutes or so to moisten it, then allow it to drain; or moisten it with a fine spray from a hand mister. In this case, make sure it is moist below the surface.

3. Tear open the seed packet and sow the seed thinly and evenly on the surface of the compost. If the seeds are large, they may be placed by hand. If they are very fine, they can be mixed with some fine sand as a carrier.

4. Cover the seed with its own depth of sieved compost, sharp sand, or Perlite or vermiculite. Make sure the covering is even. Some very fine, dust-like seeds do not need covering but should be left on the surface of the compost.

5. Place a plastic cover or a piece of glass over the sown container, and put it in a warm place, out of direct sunlight. It can be dark – light is not generally necessary for germination. Glass can be covered with a sheet of newspaper to keep in warmth.

6. Check the container regularly to make sure the compost has not dried out, and to watch for emerging seedlings. As soon as the first seedling is seen, move the container to a light place, but still out of direct sun. If you are using glass to cover the container, remove it when the first seedling is about to touch it.

Special techniques

Sometimes, some special techniques are required, in which case the seed packet will usually tell you what to do. Seeds may require pre-chilling before sowing, in which case they are mixed with moist compost and placed in a bag in the fridge for the recommended time. Some seeds have a tough seed coat which requires nicking with a knife or rubbing with sandpaper to speed up germination; other seed may need to be soaked for a short while. The seed coats of cyclamen contain an inhibitor which can be removed by soaking overnight and then washing under running water for 30 minutes.

Aftercare

Once you have successfully germinated the seed, you need to care for the seedlings. Keep them growing in the same container for a while, making sure the compost remains just moist, and the seedlings get plenty of light, but not direct sunlight, which could scorch the delicate leaves. A propagator cover with adjustable vents is useful, as it gives plenty of headroom for the plants, and the vents can be opened just the right amount to keep the air humid without too much condensation. Gradually open the vents more to acclimatize the seedlings before removing the cover.

When the seedlings are large enough to handle comfortably, or when the leaves begin to touch one another, it is time to move the seedlings on to give them more space. This is known as pricking out or pricking off. Seedlings may be moved to another tray, but spaced further apart, or they may be moved to individual pots, depending on their size. They always need very careful handling.

Use a dibber or similar tool to lift the seedlings carefully from the compost. Lever them out from well underneath, to prevent damaging too many of the young roots, and always handle them by the seed leaves, never the stem (the seed leaves are the

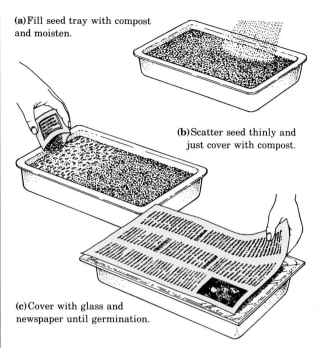

(a) Fill seed tray with compost and moisten.

(b) Scatter seed thinly and just cover with compost.

(c) Cover with glass and newspaper until germination.

Fig. 21 Sowing seeds in a container.

first leaves to emerge, and are usually a different shape and coarser than the true leaves). The stem of a seedling is very delicate and if it is bruised by handling, the seedling will collapse. It is important to sow the seed thinly, because then the seedlings can be left for longer in their original container so that they will be more robust when the time comes for pricking out.

Continue to move the young plants on to new containers as they require more space. Keep them in much the same conditions as the mature plants require, but being extra careful to protect them from direct sunlight, draughts or chills. When moving them to cooler conditions, acclimatize them gradually to prevent a sudden check to growth.

Increasing ferns

Ferns do not produce seed – they reproduce in a different way, by spores. Spores can be sown in a similar way to seeds, and while it is not a particularly easy job to raise new ferns from spores, it is an interesting process you might like to try.

The spores are produced on the undersides of the leaf, and can be seen as brown spots or stripes. When these marks are prominent, but before the spore cases have split to shed the tiny spores, cut off a leaf and place it in a paper bag. Leave it in a dry place until the spores have been shed.

Prepare a shallow plastic pan of peat-based potting compost, firm it lightly so the surface is perfectly level, and stand it in a dish of water until the surface of the compost is moist. In a draught-free room, tip the contents of the bag on to a sheet of paper and remove the remains of the leaf. The spores are a very fine, soft dust. Sprinkle them from the paper on to the surface of the compost, cover with a propagator top or inflated plastic bag, and place the pot and saucer in a warm, light place. Keep the saucer topped up with water so the compost is permanently moist.

After some weeks, the spores produce flat, green, rounded, slimy looking growths which cover the compost surface. These contain the male and female organs of the plant, and fertilization takes place at this stage instead of in the flowers, like most other plants. When the tiny ferns appear, the cover can be removed from the pan.

The ferns can be potted up first in little groups, then individually as they become larger. The whole process may take a year or more, so patience is needed.

Saving your own seed

Seed produced by flowering house plants can be saved and sown, too. Plants do not always produce seed, sometimes because conditions are not right for fertilization, or because faded flowers are removed because they are unattractive. If seed is allowed to form, however, it should be left on the plant until thoroughly ripe, then sown straight away.

Some plants raised from seed have quite different characteristics from the mature plants: their habit of growth, leaf size and shape may vary considerably. You may have to wait for a year or more before the young plants are suitable for display, but they may be mature in a matter of weeks. However long they take, there is always a special interest and pride in plants that you have raised yourself, from seed.

·EXAMPLES OF PROPAGATION METHODS·

Method	Plants	
Air layering	Cordyline Dracaena	*Ficus robusta* Monstera
Division	Chlorophytum Ferns Maranta	Saintpaulia Spathiphyllum Syngonium
Leaf cuttings	Begonia Crassula Peperomia	Saintpaulia Sansevieria Streptocarpus
Offsets	Aechmea and other bromeliads	Narcissus and other bulbs Cacti – many types
Seed	Capsicum Coleus Cyclamen Exacum	Impatiens Passiflora Pelargonium Solanum
Stem cuttings	Coleus Croton *Ficus benjamina* Hedera	Impatiens Pelargonium Pilea Tradescantia

·6·
Keeping Plants Healthy

Indoor plants, like any other, are subject to a range of pests and diseases. These can be many and varied, but they all produce a damaging or displeasing effect. As a general rule, they may slow down or stop the plant's growth, prevent flowering, or physically damage or distort parts of the plant. Pests are animals (mainly insects) that cause this damage; diseases are fungal, bacterial or virus organisms.

There is another range of problems called physiological disorders. These are not diseases because they are not caused by any disease organism; they are just things that can go wrong with the plant. There are also cultural disorders – that means problems caused by us, the plant's keeper! Overwatering, underwatering, being kept too cold, in a draught, scorched by the sun – all will produce symptoms.

Indoor plants are being kept in artificial conditions and this can make health problems worse. The natural pest controls that exist outdoors may not be available indoors. Many indoor plants come from tropical countries where a whole range of totally different natural pest controls exist that cannot be found in this country. The growth that is produced in warm, indoor conditions, perhaps with less-than-perfect light, is often soft and sappy – an ideal target for fungus diseases.

Pest outbreaks often increase at an amazingly rapid rate indoors, because warm, sheltered conditions provide an ideal environment for pests to thrive, as well as plants. It is important to check plants regularly so that action can be taken at the first signs of trouble.

Avoiding problems

You can reduce the likelihood of a major problem with pests or diseases by taking the following steps.

• Keep plants growing strongly by giving them the correct conditions of warmth, light and moisture. It won't make them less likely to be attacked, but it will make them more able to withstand an attack.

• Keep the atmosphere 'buoyant' – that is, the air should be replaced on a regular basis through adequate ventilation without draughts. Still, humid air, especially if it is cool, provides ideal conditions for fungal diseases to develop.

• Do not overfeed plants: an excess of nitrogen makes soft, sappy growth which is vulnerable to both pests and diseases.

• Isolate newly acquired plants until you are sure they are pest and disease free.

• Check plants regularly for signs of trouble. Take care to examine the undersides of the leaves, where problems often begin.

• Learn to recognize the most common pests and diseases so that you can give the correct treatment.

MAJOR PLANT PESTS

These are the pests that you are most likely to find on indoor plants.

Aphids (Fig. 22)

Commonly known as greenfly or blackfly, though they can also be other colours, such as pink and slate-blue. These small, soft creatures are able to reproduce without fertilization; in warm conditions aphids are able to start reproducing within a week of birth, so it is easy to see how rapidly colonies can build up.

Aphids feed by sucking the sap of plants, and are particularly attracted to soft young growing tips. Their feeding debilitates the plant, and can also spread virus diseases from one plant to another. Excess sugars taken in by the aphids are excreted as honeydew, a sticky substance which drips on to the foliage (and surfaces such as table tops) below. This can attract a fungus called sooty mould, which grows on the honeydew to form sooty black patches which prevent the leaves from photosynthesizing efficiently, further debilitating the plant.

• Fortunately aphids are fairly easily controlled by a range of insecticides, including derris primicarb, pyrethrum, permethrin and malathion.

Aphids, or greenfly, are one of the commonest pests of indoor plants. They are most frequently found on young growth.

Caterpillars (Fig. 22)

A variety of caterpillars – the larval stage of various insects – may affect plants, usually chewing ragged holes in leaves. Because the larval stage is the feeding stage, caterpillars have voracious appetites, and can do a great deal of damage very quickly.

The commonest culprit is the carnation tortrix moth. These are small, yellowish green caterpillars usually found at the tips of shoots, where they form a characteristic webbing, pulling the leaves of the plant together while they feed.

• For control, try trichlorphon, derris, fenitrothion and pirimiphos-methyl, which may be applied as sprays or dust formulations.

Mealy bugs (Fig. 22)

These look a bit like woodlice covered in white, waxy fluff, and can usually be found clustered in leaf axils. They are often a particular problem on cacti, when they are round the base of the spines. Although they can move about, they tend to remain immobile while feeding. Like aphids, they are sap suckers, and have the same effects of debilitating plants and secreting honeydew, attracting sooty mould.

• One method of control is to use a cotton bud dipped in methylated spirits to paint the colonies of insects. Spray thoroughly with permethrin or malathion, or the systemic insecticide dimethoate.

Red spider mite (Fig. 22)

These minute mites are related to spiders. They are scarcely visible to the naked eye, but can be seen with a hand lens. They feed on sap, and often the first symptom is a characteristic yellow speckling of the foliage. The tips of shoots are also often covered with a very fine webbing in which the tiny mites can be seen scurrying backwards and forwards by those with sharp enough eyes.

·HANDY TIP·

Small hand sprayers are ideal both for applying insecticides and fungicides to plants and misting them to create a humid atmosphere. Don't use the same sprayer for both, however; buy two and label one 'pesticides' with a spirit-based felt tip pen.

Red spider mites love hot, dry conditions, and plants can be severely damaged as numbers of mites rapidly build up. They overwinter in cracks and crannies around the plants, so the problem may persist from year to year.

• Increase the humidity round affected plants and treat with a malathion or permethrin-based insect spray.

Scale insects (Fig. 22)

Scale insects pass through various stages in their life cycle, but we usually notice them as a static grey or brown, smooth limpet-like 'scale'. They attach themselves to the stems and undersides of leaves while they feed on sap; once more they excrete honeydew which means that sooty mould very often accompanies an infestation. They are often quite difficult to spot.

• Scale insects can sometimes be scraped off with a fingernail, or can be treated with malathion, permethrin or pyrethrum.

Vine weevil

It is the larvae of this pest that cause the main problem. They live in the compost in pots, and feed happily on the roots, out of sight. Often the first sign that they are present is the collapse of the shoots and foliage. They have a particular liking for cyclamen, and will gnaw away large portions of the tuber until it can no longer support the plant.

Fig. 22 Several pests may be found on house plants: they are unlikely to occur all at the same time, but all should be dealt with swiftly.

Aphids (greenfly) are probably the commonest pest; they are easy to control, but multiply rapidly if untreated

Red spider mites, which thrive in dry atmospheres, are tiny, but their webbing can often be spotted at the tips of shoots or leaves

Mealybugs look like woodlice with a grey, fluffy coating, which tends to repel pesticide applications; try a systemic insecticide

Scale insects are difficult to spot, but they tend to occur on the undersides of leaves along the main veins

Caterpillars are not very common on indoor plants but can do a lot of damage in a short time; suspect them if you see chewed leaves

Adult whitefly look like small white moths; these persistent pests need several pesticide treatments before they are controlled

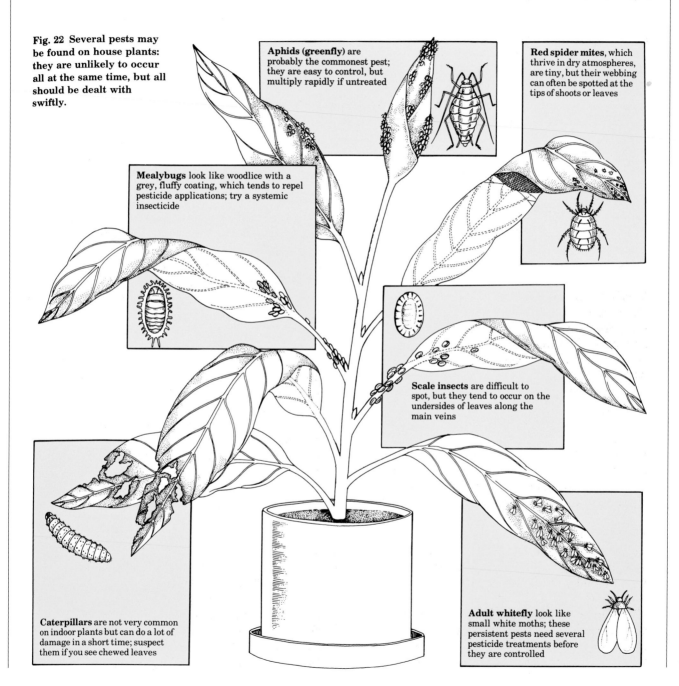

Vine weevil larvae carry out their destructive work below soil level, and often the total collapse of the plant is the first sign of trouble. Cyclamen are particularly prone to this pest.

Adult weevils sometimes eat characteristic notches out of leaf edges, and are active at night when they can sometimes be spotted by torchlight. They cannot fly, but spend the day in plant debris and nooks and crannies at soil level.
• Vine weevil damage can be prevented by mixing Gamma HCH dust with the compost when potting up.

Whitefly (Fig. 22)
Tiny, white, moth-like creatures that can rise from badly infested plants in clouds, whitefly can be a real problem to control. They pass through various stages in their life cycle, but only the adult is susceptible to pesticides. This means repeated spraying in order to catch all the different generations.

Whitefly are once again sap suckers, with the attendant problems of honeydew and sooty mould. They do reduce plant vigour, but are unlikely to seriously damage plants in themselves. The sooty mould can do more damage by reducing photosynthesis.
• Pirimphos-methyl can be used, but repeated treatments will be needed.

MAJOR PLANT DISEASES

Plant diseases are usually not as obvious as pest attacks; fungi are the major cause.

Botrytis
Usually known as grey mould, which describes it very well, botrytis is a common disease in greenhouses but not quite so common in homes. It generally starts on dead tissue such as a dead leaf or flower head, and will spread to the rest of the plant. Affected parts are covered by a fluffy grey mould growth which gives off lots of spores when the plant is handled.

When spraying plants with contact insecticides, it is important to treat the *under*sides of the leaves, where many pests lurk, not just the top surfaces.

The disease is encouraged by damp, cool conditions, so tends to be most frequent in autumn. Avoid watering plants late in the day if they are going to be subject to rapidly falling night temperatures. Plenty of ventilation to keep a buoyant atmosphere will help. Clear away all dead and dying parts of the plant as soon as they are seen, removing wilted leaves, dead flowers and so on.

61

• Use a fungicide like carbendazim or benomyl, in liquid or dust formulation, to prevent the spread of the disease.

Damping off
This fungus disease attacks seedlings, causing the stem of the plant to collapse at soil level. It will frequently sweep through a whole tray of seedlings, destroying the lot. Overcrowded conditions encourage it, so sow seeds thinly and ensure the seedlings that emerge have sufficient ventilation.
• An outbreak can be treated with a copper-based fungicide.

Mildew
There are two types of mildew, downy and powdery. The one that you are likely to come across on indoor plants is powdery mildew. The disease starts as powdery white patches which grow larger until they may cover the entire leaf surface. Foliage

Fig. 23 Pests are often found on the undersides of leaves first. When using an aerosol, maintain the correct distance as detailed on the product.

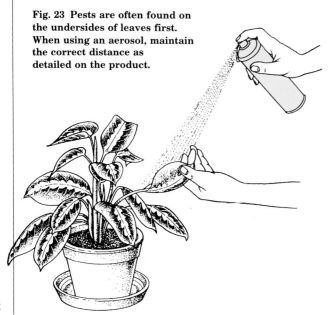

often turns yellow and falls, and the plant is obviously not thriving. Hot, dry conditions favour this disease.
• It can be treated with a range of fungicides, including carbendazim and propiconazole.

Rust
A difficult disease to control, there are several types of rust. Pelargoniums, carnations and chrysanthemums are commonly affected. The first symptom is usually a pale circular spot on the top of the leaf; on the underside is a rusty ring of brown spores.
• Affected leaves should be carefully picked off and burned and the plants treated with a fungicide containing propiconazole to prevent the disease from spreading.

Virus
Viruses give rise to a wide range of symptoms on a large number of plants. Symptoms may include mottling or mosaic patterning of foliage; malformed leaves, with curled, rolled or twisted edges, and misshapen flowers which may be green or streaked with lighter colours. Plants often affected include hippeastrums, lilies, chrysanthemums, cyclamen, carnations, pelargoniums and orchids.
• *Viruses cannot be controlled by chemicals.* They are mainly spread by aphids moving from infected to uninfected plants, so controlling aphids will help prevent viruses occurring. Infected plants should be removed and destroyed when seen.

·PLANT PROBLEMS AND CHEMICAL CONTROLS·

Pest	Controls
Aphids	derris; heptenophos & permethrin; permethrin; malathion; pirimicarb; pirimiphos methyl; pyrethrum
Caterpillars	pyrethrum; heptenophos & permethrin; permethrin
Mealy bugs	heptenophos & permethrin; dimethoate; permethrin
Red spider mite	malathion; permethrin; pirimiphos methyl
Scale insects	pyrethrum; permethrin; malathion
Vine weevil	gamma HCH
Disease	**Controls**
Botrytis	carbendazim
Damping off	copper oxychloride
Mildew	carbendazim; propiconazole
Rust	propiconazole

USING PESTICIDES

A wide range of products to help us combat pests and diseases is available, but these will only work effectively if we use them properly (Fig. 23). The most important point, but one that is frequently ignored, is to read and understand the instructions before you begin.

Different products are used against different problems, and they may not always work effectively on all plants. Some plants may be damaged by a certain pesticide, and these will be listed on the pack. It is often important to spray plants at the right stage of growth, avoiding flowering times, and when edible products are being treated there may be a harvest interval to be observed before treated produce can be eaten. Do not spray plants in bright, direct sunlight.

Chemicals should be stored in a dry place, out of the reach of children and animals. Never decant pesticides into another, unlabelled container. Use them strictly according to the instructions on the label (Fig. 24), and if the label has become illegible, dispose of the pesticide safely.

Types of pesticide
Pesticides are available in several different formulations.

• *Dusts* are useful where it is important to keep moisture levels down, but can be difficult to apply evenly.

• *Liquids* can be used as foliage sprays or for drenching the compost (Fig. 24). They are generally supplied as concentrates – either granules or powders to mix with water, or concentrated liquids for dilution – though several are now available in a convenient, ready-to-use form. For indoor plants, a

Fig. 24 Some pesticides need to be applied to the compost in order to be taken up by the plant roots.

Chemicals must be measured accurately, so never add 'a bit more for luck' as it could damage the plant

small hand mister is usually sufficient to apply the chemical. Make sure the undersides of the leaves are treated, too.

• *Aerosols* are also simple to use but care must be taken to spray plants from the recommended distances. Too close, and you may damage the foliage.

Many chemicals are very dangerous to fish, and fish tanks in the same room should be covered before any pesticides are applied to plants. Always move plants away from furniture that may be damaged by moisture before spraying with liquids or aerosols.

Some pesticides can be mixed together to control more than one problem – usually a fungicide and insecticide to control both pests and diseases with one spraying. You can mix these yourself *only* when the label specifies it: other chemicals may not be compatible. Some ready-mixed products are available.

NON-CHEMICAL CONTROLS

Some gardeners do not like to use any sort of pesticides on their plants; others prefer to use them as little as possible. There are several ways in which pests can be attacked without reaching for the sprayer. The most simple is to remove and destroy the affected part of the plant as soon as it is seen, for example a leaf with signs of botrytis, or a shoot tip infested with aphids can easily be pinched

Insecticides may be formulated as dusts as well as liquids. Dusts are puffed on to the plant, or on to the compost in the case of soil-living pests. They can be difficult to apply evenly.

64

Check plants for pests regularly. Outbreaks can often be literally 'nipped in the bud' by removing affected parts at the first sign of trouble.

out. Some pests can be removed individually; scale insects can sometimes be scraped off with a finger-nail, for instance.

Altering the environment the plants are growing in can also be used to fight pests and diseases. Red spider mite thrives in hot, dry conditions, so frequent damping down to give a moist atmosphere will help to keep it at bay. Grey mould disease (botrytis) flourishes in cool damp conditions, and turning up the heat and being careful not to splash water about unnecessarily will go a long way to avoiding this problem getting a hold.

Organic pesticides are now widely available, and these are based on natural substances such as soaps and plant extracts. Biological control works well in greenhouses.

Ensuring that a plant is growing in the ideal conditions so that it is not under stress will help to make sure that it can weather any pest or disease attack without too much damage.

·7·
Popular Foliage Plants

The following is a list of some of the plants you are most likely to come across in garden centres and shops: most of them are well-established, old favourites.

Adiantum capillus-veneris (maidenhair fern)
The delicate, fresh green, pinnate leaves, carried on slender black stems that give the maidenhair its common name, make it an attractive pot plant. It is not difficult to grow provided it receives the high humidity it needs to prevent the leaves becoming brown and crisp. Group it with other plants, or stand it on a tray of pebbles topped up with water, and mist the foliage regularly. It is an ideal subject for a bottle garden.
Light: moderate light, always out of direct sun.
Temperature: 13–18°C (55–65°F).
Water: keep the compost moist at all times; do not allow to dry out at any stage.
Propagation: division, spores.

Aechmea fasciata (urn plant)
This plant is a bromeliad, in its natural habitat living on the branches of trees. The leaves are long and spined, banded with silver scales, and form a large rosette. The flowerhead which arises from the centre is long lasting, and consists of tightly packed, bright pink bracts from which emerge pale violet flowers.
Light: bright light, not in direct sun.

Temperature: 10–18°C (50–65°F).
Water: water moderately, allowing the compost to dry out between waterings, especially at lower temperatures. Fill the 'vase' in the centre of the rosette when it dries out, preferably with rainwater.
Propagation: offsets.

Aralia elegantissima see **Dizygotheca elegantissima**

Begonia species
Begonias may be valuable for either foliage or flowers. The foliage types have striking leaves marked with various patterns and colours, and include *Begonia boweri*, with small, mid-green leaves marked with bronze towards their hairy margins; *B. masoniana* (iron cross begonia) which has medium sized, textured leaves of mid-green marked with a strong, chocolate-brown cross, and probably the best known of them all, *B. rex*. The leaves are large and unevenly heart-shaped, with strong splashes and interveinal markings of metallic pink, silver and cream. There are many different rex hybrids.
Light: good, filtered light.
Temperature: 12–18°C (54–65°F)
Water: water moderately, allowing the compost to dry out between waterings.
Propagation: leaf cuttings.

Caladium hortulanum (angels' wings)

The large, arrowhead-shaped leaves are paper thin, almost translucent, delicately marked with pink, white and cream. They are carried on long, slender stalks and die down in autumn, leaving the tuber to overwinter. This is a spectacular plant, but not an easy one to grow, being very sensitive to cold and draughts. It needs a warm, humid atmosphere.

Light: good, bright light but never in direct sunlight.

Temperature: 18–21 °C (65–70 °F) in summer, with a minimum of 16 °C (60 °F). In winter, keep the dormant tubers at 13–16 °C (55–60 °F).

Water: during the growing season, keep the compost moist at all times. Decrease in autumn as the plant dies down until the tubers are in barely-moist compost over winter.

Propagation: tuber offsets.

Calathea makoyana see **Maranta**

Chlorophytum comosum variegatum (spider plant)

One of the most popular house plants because it is so easy to grow and increase, the spider plant is nevertheless an attractive and rewarding choice. The long, grassy, yellow and green leaves arch over in a fountain of foliage, and in summer, wiry cream stems carry white flowers at their tips. The flowers are followed by baby plantlets which give a very attractive cascading effect. It is a very adaptable plant, though very dry conditions will cause the tips of the foliage to become brown.

Light: bright light, preferably out of direct sun though it will tolerate it.

Temperature: anything between 7° and 27 °C (45–80 °F) is tolerated.

Water: keep the compost moist at all times in summer, allow it to dry out between waterings in winter.

Propagation: baby plantlets root easily when detached from the mother plant.

Cissus rhombifolia see **Rhoicissus rhombifolia**

Codiaeum variegatum 'Pictum' (Joseph's coat)

The leaves are brightly coloured, spotted and splashed in shades of red, yellow, orange, green and cream – sometimes all on one leaf! They may also be of various shapes, some being entire, some lobed, some crinkled. The plant grows in a bushy, upright shape, and the lower leaves are often lost when conditions are not just right, giving a rather unattractive bare lower stem. This plant requires a humid atmosphere, particularly in high temperatures.

Light: good, bright light is required for good leaf colour, but not direct summer sun.

Temperature: minimum 15 °C (60 °F) to 24 °C (75 °F).

·PLANTS WITH VARIEGATED FOLIAGE·

Name	Description
Aglaeonema crispum 'Silver Queen'	Green and white, spear-shaped leaves
Dieffenbachia picta superba (dumb cane)	Broad, mid-green leaves marked with white
Dracaena fragrans massangeana (corn palm)	Long, broad, mid-green leaves with central gold stripe
Ficus benjamina varieties (weeping fig)	Graceful weeping trees, marked with creamy white in varying patterns
Hedera varieties (ivy)	Strong-growing climbers with leaves of varying sizes, mottled or edged grey-green, cream, white or gold
Pilea cadierei (aluminium plant)	Silver-mottled, textured leaves
Scindapsus aureus	Gold and cream, heart-shaped foliage
Syngonium podophyllum varieties (goosefoot)	Arrow-shaped or lobed gold- or cream-splashed leaves

Water: keep the compost moist at all times in spring and summer; allow the surface to dry out between watering in autumn and winter.
Propagation: soft stem cuttings in spring; bare-stemmed plants can be air layered.

Coleus blumei (flame nettle)

The leaves of the coleus are brilliantly coloured in shades of fiery red, brilliant orange, yellow, bronze, old gold, lime-green, rose pink and deep maroon. Some varieties have lacy edges to the foliage.

The tips of the quick-growing shoots should be regularly pinched out to maintain a bushy shape, or the plant becomes unattractively leggy. Soft stem cuttings should be taken so that mother plants can be thrown away when they become too ungainly. Flowers are rather insignificant and are usually pinched out.
Light: good, bright light is essential for good colour.
Temperature: 10–18°C (50–65°F).
Water: keep the compost just moist at all times.
Propagation: soft stem suttings and seed.

Cyperus

Cyperus is the plant to grow if you have trouble watering your house plants correctly; it requires a permanent supply of moisture at the roots and cannot be overwatered! The tall stems are topped by umbrellas of radiating bracts that look like leaves (the true leaves clasp the stem closely and are hardly visible) giving the plant an oriental appearance. *C. diffusus* (umbrella plant) is a shorter, stockier plant than *C. alternifolius*. Leaf tips become brown if the roots become dry at any stage.

◄ **Angels wings, or *Caladium hortulanum*, is not the easiest of plants to grow but is certainly one of the most spectacular.**

Light: moderate to good, indirect light.
Temperature: 13–20°C (55–70°F).
Water: keep the compost saturated at all times; the pot can stand in a saucer of water which is kept topped up. Ideal for hydroculture.
Propagation: division; or cut off one of the 'umbrellas' and invert it in a glass of water. New plantlets will form from the centre.

Dieffenbachia (dumbcane, leopard lily)

A popular plant with attractively marked leaves, the dumb cane is quite easy to grow. Take care as the sap is poisonous, causing unpleasant swelling and burning of the skin, especially near the mouth and eyes. *D. amoena* is a larger plant, with mid-green leaves marbled creamy yellow: *D. picta (D. maculata)* is the most commonly seen, with heavily speckled and splashed cream and green foliage. Older plants may develop leggy, bare lower stems as lower leaves are lost in dry conditions.
Light: good, bright, filtered light.
Temperature: 15–21°C (60–70°F).
Water: keep the compost just moist, allowing the surface to dry out slightly between waterings.
Propagation: stem cuttings from leggy plants can be rooted in a propagator.

Dizygotheca elegantissima, Aralia elegantissima (false aralia)

The dark foliage of dizygotheca makes it an interesting house plant. Palmate leaves are carried on tall stems, and are divided into 10 or so slender, saw-edged leaflets. Colour is a deep, coppery green and may be almost black on some plants.
Light: moderate to good light.
Temperature: 15–21°C (60–70°F).
Water: keep the compost just moist, allowing the surface to dry out between waterings.
Propagation: soft stem cuttings in a propagator; seed.

Dracaena

Most dracaenas look like palms, with long, slender leaves which may be striped with contrasting colours. The dragon tree or Ti plant is *Dracaena terminalis*: one of the most popular varieties is 'Rededge', whose green leaves are edged with rosy red. *Dracaena marginata* has a slender trunk bearing clusters of long, thin leaves with a red margin: the long, stiff, sword-like leaves of *D. deremensis* are usually variegated with cream or creamy white, and *D. sanderiana* (ribbon plant) has leaves which are not as stiff as the others, and are broadly edged with white.

Light: moderate to good light, out of direct sun.
Temperature: 15–21 °C (60–70 °F).
Water: keep the compost moist, allowing the surface to dry out between waterings in the winter.
Propagation: air layering, stem cuttings.

Fatshedera lizei (tree ivy)

This plant is a hybrid between two other plants – fatsia (castor oil plant) and hedera (ivy). It forms a bushy plant with medium to large, palmate, ivy-like leaves which are often attractively variegated.
Light: good, bright light.
Temperature: 10–18 °C (50–65 °F).
Water: keep the compost just moist, allowing the surface to dry out between waterings, especially in the winter.
Propagation: stem cuttings in spring and summer.

Ficus (Fig. 25)

The rubber plant family give us so many attractive and reliable indoor plants, some of them very different from each other. The weeping fig (*Ficus benjamina*) is one of the most popular of all house plants, with its graceful, weeping, tree-fern form. Several variegated varieties are available. The india rubber plant (*Ficus elastica*) is a long-standing favourite, with broad, leathery leaves

Fig. 25 The rubber plant family, ficus, provides a wide range of different plant forms: (a) *Ficus lyrata* (b) *Ficus pumila*, and (c) *Ficus benjamina*.

which may be deep green or, less commonly, variegated. This plant tends to go bare at the base as it gets older. Rather more attractive is *Ficus lyrata*, the fiddle-leaved fig: it is similar in habit, but with more interesting, violin-shaped leaves. Completely different are two trailing types, *Ficus radicans* (trailing fig) and *F. pumila* (creeping fig). These have small leaves and wiry, trailing stems; they need humid conditions.

Light: moderate to good light. The trailing kinds must be kept out of direct sunshine at all times.
Temperature: 15–24 °C (60–75 °F).
Water: keep the compost just moist, allowing it to dry out between waterings. The trailing types like moister conditions than the tree types.
Propagation: soft stem cuttings or air-layering (tree types).

·HANDY TIP·

Variegated plants sometimes produce a plain-leaved shoot which tends to grow more strongly and will soon swamp the plant. Cut out non-typical shoots as soon as they are seen.

Fittonia (snakeskin plant)
This trailing plant is ideal for a bottle garden or terrarium, as it loves moist, humid conditions. The rounded leaves are delicately marked with a network of red (*F. verschaffeltii*) or silver (*F. argyroneura*). The dwarf variety. *F. argyroneura* 'Nana' will put up with drier air.
Light: partial shade; never direct sun.
Temperature: 15–21 °C (60–70 °F).
Water: keep the compost moist during the growing season; allow it to dry out slightly between waterings in winter.
Propagation: stem cuttings or division.

Hedera (ivy)
Ivy is a fast-growing, easy-to-please climber which can be trained up supports or a wall, or will trail from a hanging pot. There is a good variety of leaf shapes and colours. *H. helix* has leaves of a typical ivy shape, variegated with gold, cream, and dark and light green in many different patterns. *H. canariensis* is larger-leaved; the most common variety is 'Gloire de Marengo', with cream-edged, mottled grey-green foliage. Ivies are prone to attack by red spider mite in warm, dry air: they like cool conditions. Mist regularly with plain water.
Light: good, bright light. Will stand some direct sunlight but best shielded from midsummer sun.
Temperature: 7–15 °C (45–60 °F).
Water: keep the compost moist at all times, allowing the surface to dry out very slightly between waterings.
Propagation: stem cuttings.

Heptapleurum arboricola (parasol plant)
A branching, tree-like plant, umbrella-like leaves with about 10 leaflets on each leaf stalk. Variegated varieties, splashed with gold, are most commonly seen. It requires moist, humid air.
Light: good light, out of direct sun.
Temperature: 15–20 °C (60–67 °F).
Water: keep the compost moist in summer; allow to dry out slightly between waterings in winter.
Propagation: stem cuttings.

·TRAILING PLANTS·	
Name	**Description**
Asparagus fern (*Asparagus densiflorus sprengeri*)	Wiry stems with bristly foliage that cascades over the pot; keep moist and humid, or the needle-like leaves will fall
Columnea (*Columnea banksii*)	Cascading stems with shiny leaves and yellow and red tubular flowers
Devil's ivy (*Scindapsus aureus*)	Heart-shaped leaves, often heavily variegated; vigorous grower
Ivy (*Hedera helix*)	Many varieties of ivy succeed well indoors; the variegated types are particularly attractive
Mouther-of-thousands (*Saxifraga sarmentosa*)	Produces trails of baby plantlets; rounded, hairy leaves veined silver
Spider plant (*Chlorophytum comosum*)	Very easy; grassy leaves and cascades of baby plantlets on long arching stems
Swedish ivy (*Plectranthus oertendahlii*)	Rounded, mid-green leaves with the veins picked out in white; easy to grow
Sweetheart plant (*Philodendron scandens*)	Heart-shaped, glossy leaves on a vigorous plant
Velvet plant (*Gynura sarmentosa*)	Velvety stems and shoots covered in fine purple hairs
Wandering Jew (*Tradescantia fluminensis*)	Soft, trailing stems with clasping, silver, pointed leaves; very easy to grow from cuttings

◄ The stiff, sharply pointed leaves of *Dracaena deremensis* are generally variegated: this variety is 'Lemon & Lime'. The plants need moderate to good light, but not direct sun.

► The polka dot plant, *Hypoestes sanguinolenta*, is brightly freckled with pink spots. Plants tend to become unattractively leggy rather quickly.

Howea forsteriana (kentia palm)
One of the easiest palms, which will put up with less than ideal conditions. The divided leaves give the plant a feathery appearance. They grow on a short trunk, making this a good specimen plant. Moist air is necessary to prevent the leaf tips turning brown.
Light: moderate to good light.
Temperature: 13–18°C (55–65°F).
Water: water sparingly in winter; in summer keep the compost just moist, allowing the surface to dry out between waterings.
Propagation: seed.

Hypoestes sanguinolenta (polka dot plant)
This is a like-it or loathe-it plant. The soft, more-or-less rounded leaves are blotched and freckled with many pink spots; flowers are insignificant. Plants tend to become leggy with time, and though they are often planted in bottle gardens, they are not ideal for this, as they soon outgrow their space.
Light: bright light is necessary for good leaf colour. Will stand some direct sunlight.
Temperature: 15–21°C (60–70°F).
Water: keep the compost moist, allowing the surface to dry out in winter.
Propagation: stem cuttings.

73

Maranta (prayer plant, peacock plant)
Marantas are popular with boldly coloured leaves; **Maranta leuconeura kershoveana** is blotched chocolate brown, while *M. tricolor* has veins prominently marked in red. The leaves, on semi-trailing stems, fold up at night, which gives the plants their common name of prayer plant. *Calathea makoyana* has a similar shaped leaf, very thin, with bold, peacock's tail-like markings. It requires more humid, warmer conditions than the true marantas.
Light: moderate to good light, out of direct sun.
Temperature: 13–18 °C (55–65 °F) for marantas, 15–20 °C (60–68 °F) for calatheas.
Water: keep compost moist through the growing season; allow the surface to dry out between waterings in winter.
Propagation: division.

Monstera deliciosa (Swiss cheese plant)
The common name of this plant arises from the irregular holes which appear in leaves as they mature: they begin life entire and heart-shaped and end up large, glossy and deeply cut. Monsteras are climbers which should be provided with a sturdy support (Fig. 26). They can outgrow a normal living room.
Light: moderate, out of direct sun.
Temperature: 16–24 °C (60–75 °F).
Water: keep the compost just moist.
Propagation: air layering.

Peperomia
Good plants for bottle gardens (Fig. 27), but also undemanding for any living areas. The foliage of *P. caperata* and *P. hederafolia* is attractively textured and corrugated: club-like, green flower spikes arise on tall stalks from the foliage. *Peperomia argyreia* has smooth leaves with silver and green stripes, while *Peperomia magnoliaefolia* is more upright

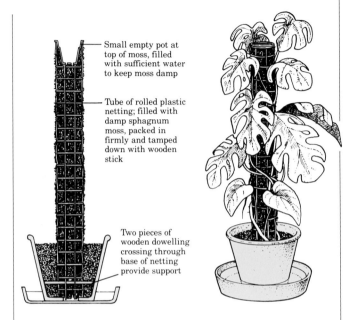

Small empty pot at top of moss, filled with sufficient water to keep moss damp

Tube of rolled plastic netting; filled with damp sphagnum moss, packed in firmly and tamped down with wooden stick

Two pieces of wooden dowelling crossing through base of netting provide support

Fig. 26 How to make a moss pole for a monstera.

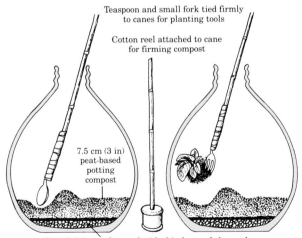

Teaspoon and small fork tied firmly to canes for planting tools

Cotton reel attached to cane for firming compost

7.5 cm (3 in) peat-based potting compost

3 cm (1 in) gravel topped with thin layer of charcoal

Fig. 27 Peperomias are ideal for bottle gardens (p.34). For narrow-necked bottles, make your own planting tools.

growing, with smooth, fleshy, variegated leaves. All the plants remain compact.

Light: bright or moderate light, out of direct sun.

Temperature: 13–18°C (55–65°F).

Water: keep the compost just moist, allowing it to dry out between waterings, especially in the winter.

Propagation: stem or leaf stem cuttings.

Philodendron

The climbing philodendron, *P. scandens* (sweetheart plant), is the better known type. It has glossy, deep green, heart-shaped leaves on strong stems which produce aerial roots: it is best trained up a moss pole or similar support. It is an undemanding plant which will do well in most conditions. *Philodendron bipinnatifidum* looks rather like a monstera; the leaves are large and very deeply cut. This type does not climb. It can grow very large, and makes a good specimen plant where there is sufficient space for it.

Light: moderate light.

Temperature: 13–18°C (55–65°F).

Water: keep the compost moist through the growing season; allow the surface to dry out between waterings in the winter.

Propagation: air layering (climbers), stem cuttings (non-climbers).

Pilea cadieri (aluminium plant)

A compact, bushy plant, with pointed leaves splashed with a metallic silver. Pinch out the growing tips to keep the plant bushy, and take cuttings to replace plants when they become too leggy.

Light: bright, indirect light.

Temperature: 13–21°C (55–70°F).

Water: keep the compost just moist, allowing the surface to dry out between waterings.

Propagation: stem cuttings.

Radermachera sinica

A fairly recent introduction, which has become very popular and widely available. It is tree-like in form, with attractive, glossy, mid-green leaves divided into leaflets. It generally remains fairly compact and is easy to look after.

Light: good, bright light out of direct sun.

Temperature: 16–20°C (60–70°F).

Water: keep the compost moist throughout the growing season, allowing it to dry out between waterings in the winter.

Propagation: seed.

Rhoicissus rhomboidea, Cissus rhombifolia
(grape ivy)

This plant quickly makes a soft, green screen when trained up a trellis. The leaves are lobed, similar to those of a grape vine, and a fresh, light green. It is an easy plant to care for, and grows rapidly. Be sure to provide adequate support for the young climbing shoots.

Light: moderate to good light, out of direct sun.

Temperature: 10–18°C (50–65°F).

Water: keep the compost moist, allowing the surface to dry out between waterings.

Propagation: soft stem cuttings.

Sanseviera trifasciata (mother-in-law's tongue)

The foliage of the plant is sharp (hence the common name) and spiky: the narrow, sword-like leaves

Saintpaulias are good-tempered plants that will flower throughout the year if sufficient light is available. The flowers come in a wide range of colours.

grow straight up and form a good specimen plant. The most popular variety is 'Laurentii', which has golden borders to the grey-green banded leaves. 'Hahnii' is quite different, with much shorter leaves growing in a rosette; it looks something like an aechmea.

Light: very adaptable – moderate light to bright sun.

Temperature: 15–24 °C (60–75 °F).

Water: water sparingly, allowing the compost to dry out between waterings.

Propagation: leaf cuttings or offsets.

Scindapsus aureus (devil's ivy, pothos)

This is a trailer or climber which will do well trained on a moss pole: it forms aerial roots. The leaves are leathery and heart shaped, often brightly variegated, though the strongly variegated types are more difficult to care for.

Light: moderate to bright light out of direct summer sun; variegated varieties need good light to keep their markings.

Temperature: 13–18 °C (55–65 °F).

Water: keep the compost moist in summer, allowing the surface to dry out between waterings; water sparingly in winter.

Propagation: stem cuttings.

Syngonium podophyllum (goosefoot plant)

The young leaves start off shaped like an arrowhead: as they mature they become lobed. Variegated varieties are most popular. If allowed to grow large enough, the plants will start to climb and can be given a moss pole.

Light: moderate to bright light, out of direct sun. Variegated varieties require bright light to retain their markings.

Temperature: 15–20°C (60–68°F).

Water: keep the compost moist at all times.

Propagation: stem cuttings.

Tradescantia (wandering Jew) (Fig. 25)

This is a very popular plant because it is so easy to grow and propagate. It is a trailing plant with elongated, oval leaves clasping the soft, fleshy stems. Leaves are usually variegated or striped silver and green. The leaves often have pink-purple undersides. The different species (*Tradescantia albiflora*, *T. blossfeldiana*, *T. fluminensis*) are all quite similar in appearance.

Light: moderate to bright light.

Temperature: 15–18°C (60–65°F).

Water: keep the compost just moist at all times.

Propagation: stem cuttings.

Yucca

Often offered for sale as one or two rosettes of stiff, mid-green, sword-like leaves on a stout, flat-topped 'trunk', yuccas are very tolerant indoor plants, though they are an acquired taste. They can reach 3 m (10 ft) tall, when they make good achitectural specimens; they are inclined to be top-heavy and need large pots, preferably filled with a loam-based compost, to balance the top growth. *Yucca aloifolia* has very sharp-pointed leaves: *Y. elephantipes* is more popular as a house plant.

Light: good, bright light, with direct sun.

Temperature: 10–20°C (50–70°F).

Water: keep the compost just moist in summer, allowing the surface to dry out between waterings. Water sparingly in winter.

Propagation: cuttings, offsets.

The narrow, very tall, spiky leaves of mother-in-law's tongue make it a good specimen plant. 'Laurentii' is the best known form, with gold-bordered foliage.

·8·
Popular Flowering Plants

Achimenes hybrids (hot water plants)
Achimenes grow from small, scaly rhizomes, producing lax growth with small, oval, dark green leaves. The flowers are freely produced in summer and autumn, and are trumpet-shaped with flat, pansy-like faces. Colours range from purple, through pinks and salmon to white, and flowers may have contrasting coloured veins or eyes. Plants become dormant in late autumn, dying back to the rhizomes.
Light: good, bright light. Will stand some direct sun but not too much strong summer sun.
Temperature: 7–20°C (45–68°F).
Water: keep the compost moist at all times when the plants are growing strongly, using tepid water. Decrease watering as they begin to die down, and store rhizomes in the pots in dry soil over winter.
Propagation: new rhizomes produced each year.

Aphelandra squarrosa (zebra plant, pineapple plant)
The bold, white veins on deep green, shiny leaves give this plant one of its common names: the other comes from the tall flowerhead, which is composed of yellow bracts flushed with red, from which yellow, tubular flowers emerge. The flowerhead remains attractive for several weeks; if it is cut back as it begins to die, new flowers are sometimes produced from lower down the plant.

Light: bright light, but not direct sun.
Temperature: 15–24°C (60–75°F).
Water: keep the compost moist at all times.
Propagation: stem cuttings.

Begonia species
Several types of begonia make good indoor plants. The wax begonia, *B. semperflorens,* is often used for bedding, and plants that have been bedded out can be potted up before the first frosts and brought inside to continue their display. *Begonia tuberhybrida* is also used outside, especially in tubs and hanging baskets. The flowers are large and may be single or rosette-like double, in red, pink, white yellow or orange.

Begonia lucerna has long, roughly heart-shaped, white-spotted leaves and pendulous bunches of pink flowers, while *B. coccinea* has narrower, mid-green leaves margined with red. Both these begonias are tall plants, and belong to a group known as 'cane begonias'.
Light: bright light; most types will stand direct sun but the cane begonias are better shielded from it.
Temperature: 10–20°C (50–68°F).
Water: keep the compost just moist, allowing the surface to dry out slightly between waterings.
Propagation: stem cuttings. Tubers can be divided with a sharp knife, ensuring each section has a growth bud.

·EARLY-FLOWERING BULBS FOR INDOORS·

Name and variety	Description
Crocus	
• *Large-flowered*	
'Pickwick'	Pale lilac striped silver
'Queen of the Blues'	Silvery mauve
• *Crocus Chrysanthus*	
'E. P. Bowles'	Yellow, feathered with chocolate brown
Hyacinth	
'Anne Marie'	Soft pink
'Bismarck'	Cornflower blue
'Jan Bos'	Rich red
• *Multiflora*	
'Borah'	Several loose, delicate spikes of pale blue
'Rosalie'	Similar to 'Borah' but soft pink
Narcissus	
'Paperwhite'	Very free flowering; bunches of small white, scented flowers
'Grand Soleil d'Or'	Similar to 'Paperwhite' but deep yellow with orange cup
• *Miniatures*	
'Tete-a-Tete'	Lemon yellow with orange cup; several flowers per stem
'Jack Snipe'	White with pale yellow cup
Tulips	
• *Tulipa Kauffmanniana*	
'Stress'	Yellow wih red splash; mottled leaves
'Johann Strauss'	Cream flushed rose-red
• *Tulipa Greigii*	
'Plaisir'	Red with creamy edge
'Cape Cod'	Yellow with bold red stripe.
• *Lily-flowered*	
'China Pink'	Tall; delicate rose-pink
'Golden Duchess'	Large, deep yellow

Calceolaria herbeohybrida (slipper flower)

The curiously formed, inflated pouch-like flowers give this plant its common name. Leaves are large, light green and softly downy: flowers are carried on tall stems clear of the foliage and are available in bright shades of yellow, orange and red. The pouches of the flowers are often spotted. These plants are best treated as temporary, and discarded when the flowers are over – they are very difficult to keep for another year.

Light: bright light, but out of direct sun.
Temperature: 10–15°C (50–60°F).
Water: keep the compost moist at all times.
Propagation: seed.

Capsicum annuum (Christmas pepper)

Despite the name, these plants may also be found bearing their colourful fruits in summer, though winter is the most popular season for them in the shops.

The leaves are deep green and pointed, and fruits are cone-shaped, held upright, changing from green to red or orange through yellow as they mature.

Christmas peppers like a humid atmosphere, so mist them regularly with plain water.

Light: bright light, with some direct sun.
Temperature: 13–18°C (55–65°F).
Water: keep the compost moist at all times.
Propagation: seed.

Chrysanthemun

The chrysanthemum is one of our most popular indoor plants. Recent growing techniques have given us 'pot mums' – plants which remain dwarf, carry lots of flowers, and can be had in bloom all year round. Flowers are usually double, but single varieties are also available; they come in all shades except blue.

Light: bright light with some direct sun.
Temperature: 10–16°C (50–60°F).
Water: keep the compost moist at all times.
Propagation: not practical to produce indoor plants, but stem cuttings can be taken to produce garden plants.

Cineraria see Senecio cruentus

Citrus mitis (calamondin orange)
This dwarf orange carries fragrant white flowers in summer and sporadically throughout the year; they are followed by small bitter oranges. These start off green and very gradually ripen to orange. The pointed leaves are a glossy deep green.

Citrus are good plants for conservatories, and they like to spend some time outdoors on warm days in summer. Watch out for attacks by scale insects.
Light: good, bright light with some direct sun.
Temperature: 13–18 °C (55–65 °F).
Water: keep the compost just moist, allowing the surface to dry out between waterings. Water more sparingly in winter.
Propagation: stem cuttings.

Clivia miniata (kaffir lily)
The deep green, long, narrow, strap-shaped leaves grow in a way that makes the base of this plant look rather like a leek. New leaves arise in pairs from the centre of the plant, and in spring, a tall, stout stem carries a rounded head of trumpet-shaped, orange flowers that make a spectacular display. Varieties with yellow or red flowers are also sometimes available.

Do not repot this plant until it is almost bursting out of its container, as it flowers best when pot bound. When the leaves begin to die down in autumn, the plant should be given a rest in a cool place or it will fail to flower the following year. Clivias are sometimes prone to attacks by mealy bug in the folds of the leaves.
Light: good light, but not in direct sun.
Temperature: 13–18 °C (55–65 °F) in the growing season; about 8 °C (47 °F) for the winter rest.
Water: keep the compost just moist during spring and summer. In winter, water very sparingly, allowing the compost to dry out between waterings.
Propagation: seed.

Columnea (goldfish plant)
These trailing plants make spectacular hanging baskets, but are not the easiest plants to grow in the home. The cascading stems bear small, dark green leaves in opposite pairs, and hooded, scarlet flowers. **Columnea banksii** is rather easier to grow than **C. gloriosa**: the plants are quite similar, but *C. gloriosa* has downy, deeper coloured leaves and is less spreading. There are also several named hybrids that make good house plants.
Light: bright light but not direct sun.
Temperature: 18–27 °C (65–80 °F).
Water: keep the compost just moist during the growing season. Water more sparingly in winter.
Propagation: stem cuttings.

Cyclamen persicum
Rounded, heart-shaped leaves are marked with silver and pale green. Flower stalks rise above the foliage, bearing delicate flowers with swept-back petals, in shades of red, pink, purple and white. The flowers are often delicately scented. Plants come in a range of sizes, from over 30 cm (12 in) across to miniature varieties of less than 15 cm (6 in) across, with flowers scaled down to match.

As the leaves die down, the pots should be dried out and turned on their sides until late summer or early autumn, when the tubers can be repotted.

Vine weevil larvae often attack the tubers, leading to the sudden and complete collapse of the plant.
Light: as bright a position as possible, but protected from direct, strong sunlight.
Temperature: 10–15 °C (50–60 °F).
Water: keep the compost just moist through the growing season, and avoid getting the top of the tuber wet. Keep quite dry during the rest period.
Propagation: seed. Large tubers can be cut into sections with a sharp knife, making sure there is a growth bud on each section.

Aphelandra squarrosa provides a double bonus of dark, glossy leaves boldly veined with white, and striking, yellow, long-lasting flowerheads.

81

Exacum affine (Persian violet, Arabian violet)
These are small neat plants with glossy, pointed leaves and cheerful, star-shaped purple flowers with gold centres. The flowers are attractively perfumed. Remove faded flowers to extend the flowering season, and discard plants once flowering is over.
Light: good, bright light, out of direct sun.
Temperature: 13–20 °C (55–68 °F).
Water: keep the compost moist at all times.
Propagation: seed.

·FLOWER COLOUR SPECTRUM·

Red and pink

Amaryllis (*Hippeastrum* hybrids)	Pelargonium (*Pelargonium domesticum*)
Begonia (*Begonia* hybrids)	Poinsettia (*Euphorbia pulcherrima*)
Cyclamen (*Cyclamen persicum*)	Pot chrysanth (*Chrysanthemum morifolium*)
Fuchsia (*Fuchsia hybrida*)	
Painter's Palette (*Anthurium andreanum*)	Primrose (*Primula acualis*)

Orange and yellow

Calceolaria (*Calceolaria herbeohybrida*)	Kaffir lily (*Clivia miniata*)
Cock's comb (*Celosia plumosa*)	Pot chrysanth (*Chrysanthemum morifolium*)
Genista (*Cytisus racemosus*)	Primrose (*Primula acaulis*)

Blue and purple

African violets (*Saintpaulia* hybrids)	Cineraria (*Senecio hybridus*)
Cape primrose (*Streptocarpus* hybrids)	Persian violet (*Exacum affine*)
	Primrose (*Primula acaulis*)

White and cream

African violet (*Saintpaulia* hybrids)	Pelargonium (*Pelargonium domesticum*)
Gardenia (*Gardenia jasminoides*)	Pot chrysanth (*Chrysanthemum morifolium*)
Jasmine (*Jasminum officinale*)	Primrose (*Primula acaulis*)
Peace lily (*Spathiphyllum wallisii*)	Stephanotis (*Stephanotis floribunda*)

·HANDY TIP·

Faded flowers are usually removed from flowering plants regularly; this helps to avoid fungal diseases which can begin on dead material and spread to living growth. The flowers should be left in place, however, where berries or attractive seedheads follow, or if seed is wanted for propagation.

Fuchsia hybrids
The leaves are mid green and pointed on branching stems; flowers are pendulous and bell shaped, with a range of forms (Fig. 28). Colours include pink, white, red and purple; there are hundreds of different named cultivars available.

Plants may be of a bushy or trailing habit, and can be trained into standards which are particularly suitable for conservatories. Pinch out the tips of shoots regularly to maintain a good shape. Give the plants a winter rest in a cool, frost-free place.
Light: good light with some direct sun.
Temperature: 10–16 °C (50–60 °F).
Water: keep the compost just moist through the growing season. Water very sparingly during the winter rest period.
Propagation: stem cuttings, seed.

Gardenia jasminoides
The waxy white flowers of the gardenia are one of the most deliciously scented of all indoor plants, but unfortunately this is a difficult plant to grow well. The foliage is deep green and glossy, and the plant is compact and branching. Flowers are creamy white, double or semi-double, and formed like a rose. High humidity is necessary, and the plant should be misted frequently (Fig. 29). Gardenias are lime haters, so pot them in ericaceous compost and use rainwater for watering if possible in hard water areas.

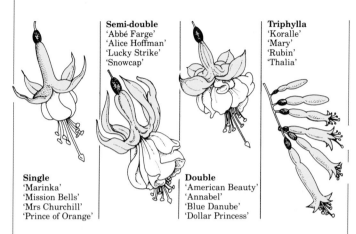

Semi-double
'Abbé Farge'
'Alice Hoffman'
'Lucky Strike'
'Snowcap'

Triphylla
'Koralle'
'Mary'
'Rubin'
'Thalia'

Single
'Marinka'
'Mission Bells'
'Mrs Churchill'
'Prince of Orange'

Double
'American Beauty'
'Annabel'
'Blue Danube'
'Dollar Princess'

Fig. 28 Different types of fuchsia flower.

Light: good, bright light, out of direct sun.
Temperature: 15–24 °C (60–75 °F).
Water: keep the compost moist through the growing period, but allow the surface to dry out between waterings in the winter.
Propagation: stem cuttings.

Hippeastrum hybrids (amaryllis)

These large bulbs are popular Christmas gifts. A tall flower spike is usually produced before the long, strap-like leaves, though they may be produced together. Flamboyant, large, trumpet-shaped flowers occur in groups of three or four, in shades of red, pink and white; they may be edged or flushed with a contrasting colour, or striped. Give the bulbs a rest period after the leaves die down, starting them into growth again in late winter or early spring.
Light: good, bright light.
Temperature: 15–21 °C (60–70 °F).
Water: keep the compost just moist through the growing season. Reduce watering as the leaves die down, and store the bulbs on their sides in dry compost for the rest period.
Propagation: offsets.

Hoya (wax plant)

Hoyas are trailing or climbing plants with showy, fragrant, waxy flowers. *Hoya carnosa* is the easiest to grow. It is a vigorous climber with twining stems that should be provided with support in the form of a trellis or similar. Leaves are pointed and fleshy; fragrant flowers are carried in clustered heads and are white with a purple centre. *Hoya bella* is a spreading trailer with similar flowers; it needs rather warmer conditions.

The faded flowerheads of hoyas should not be removed, as subsequent flowers spring from the same stalk.
Light: bright light, with some direct sun for *H. carnosa.*
Temperature: 10–21 °C (50–70 °F).
Water: keep the compost moist all through the summer. Water sparingly in winter.
Propagation: stem cuttings.

Fig. 29 Gardenias require a humid atmosphere. Stand the plants on a dish of moist pebbles and mist the foliage frequently with plain water.

83

◄ The fruits of the Christmas pepper, *Caosicum annuum*, appear in an attractive mixture of shades of green, yellow, orange and red as they ripen.

► Their pleasant sweet perfume makes the star-shaped flowers of the Persian violet (*Exacum affine*) very popular. Plants are best discarded once flowering is over.

Impatiens walleriana (busy lizzie)
The light green leaves of busy lizzies are set on fleshy, succulent stems: flat-faced, spurred flowers are carried in profusion in shades of red, pink, white and salmon. Some double-flowered and bi-coloured varieties are available. Plants are best discarded after flowering.
Light: bright light, but need to avoid direct summer sun.
Temperature: 13–18°C (55–65°F).
Water: keep the compost moist throughout the summer.
Propagation: stem cuttings, seed.

Jasminum polyanthum (jasmine)
A vigorous climber grown for its very sweetly scented, white, winter flowers. The leaves are divided into small, pointed leaflets, and are carried on slender, twining stems. Flowers are star-shaped and carried in clusters. Train the stems round a hoop or similar support (Fig. 30). Prune the stems hard after flowering to keep the plant a manageable size.
Light: bright light with some direct sun.
Temperature: 8–16°C (47–60°F).
Water: keep the compost just moist.
Propagation: stem cuttings.

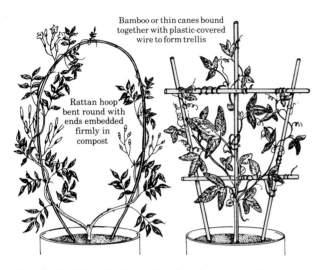

Bamboo or thin canes bound together with plastic-covered wire to form trellis

Rattan hoop bent round with ends embedded firmly in compost

Fig. 30 Climbing plants such as jasmine and passion flower need support. Use hoops or trellis.

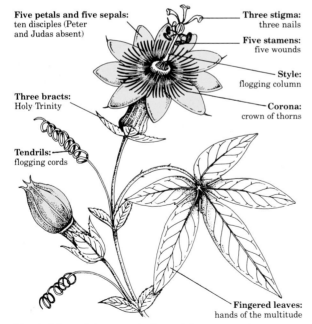

Five petals and five sepals: ten disciples (Peter and Judas absent)

Three stigma: three nails

Five stamens: five wounds

Three bracts: Holy Trinity

Style: flogging column

Corona: crown of thorns

Tendrils: flogging cords

Fingered leaves: hands of the multitude

Fig. 31 The religious symbolism of the passion flower.

Passiflora caerulea (passion flower) (Fig. 31)

The passion flower is a vigorous climber with palmate leaves and striking flowers in shades of white, purple and blue, with prominent stamens. Train plant on trellis (Fig. 30), and cut back hard each spring to keep it a manageable size.
Light: good, bright light with some direct sun.
Temperature: 8–16°C (47–60°F).
Water: keep the compost moist at all times.
Propagation: stem cuttings, seed.

Pelargonium (geranium) (Fig. 32)

Regal pelargoniums (*P. domesticum*) have fairly large, soft leaves and heads of funnel-shaped flowers whose petals have a darker eye; zonal pelargoniums (*P. zonale*) have rounder leaves with a pronounced dark 'zone' and slightly smaller flowers, while ivy-leaved varieties (*P. peltatum*) have smoother, rather brittle, roughly ivy-shaped leaves and trailing stems. All have flowers in a range of red, pink, salmon, purple, rose and white.
Light: bright light with some direct sun.
Temperature: 7–18°C (45–65°F).
Water: keep the compost just moist during the growing season, allowing the surface to dry out between waterings. Water sparingly in winter – just enough to prevent the compost drying out.
Propagation: stem cuttings, seed.

Primula (primrose)

Primroses (*P. acaulis*) are easy to grow and available in a wide range of colours. They make cheerful winter and early spring pot plants and can be planted out in the garden after flowering. *Primula malacoides* is a delicate plant with small fragrant flowers in shades of red, pink or white: it is commonly known as the fairy primrose. *P. obconica* has rather coarse, pale green leaves which can cause a severe skin rash on certain people, so care must be taken when handling this plant. The

·HANDY TIP·

A group of flowering plants can be made even more effective by arranging it carefully in front of a mirror, thus doubling the display.

flower spike of the Chinese primrose (*P. sinensis*) has small, usually frilly-edged flowers in tiers: flowers are in the usual red and pink shades, but with a distinct yellow eye.
Light: good light with some direct sun.
Temperature: 10–16°C (50–60°F).
Water: keep the compost moist at all times while flowering.
Propagation: seed.

Saintpaulia hybrids (African violet)

These cheerful plants flower all the year round if they have enough light. Rosettes of round, hairy leaves are usually dark green: variegated varieties are harder to find but can be spectacular. Flowers are held in bunches above the foliage and may be purple, pink, blue, red or white. The original flowers were violet shaped, but several different forms are now available, including doubles and frilled-edge types. Stand plants on trays of moist pebbles or similar to provide a humid atmosphere. Foliage can be misted with a very fine spray in hot summer weather only.
Light: good bright light but out of direct sun. Responds well to artificial light in winter.
Temperature: 15–21°C (60–70°F).
Water: keep the compost just moist, allowing the surface to dry out between waterings. Take care to keep water off the foliage, especially in the crown.
Propagation: division, leaf stem cuttings.

Senecio cruentus, S. hybridus (cineraria)

Daisy-like blooms in a range of colours including blue, red, pink, purple and white make these attractive, if short-lived, indoor plants. The heart-shaped leaves are soft and downy, and flowers are carried in large numbers. They are usually single, but double varieties and bicolours are also available. Plants are best discarded after flowering. Both under and overwatering will cause the plants to collapse very quickly.
Light: good light, out of direct sun.
Temperature: 10–16°C (50–60°F).
Water: keep the compost just moist at all times, but take care never to waterlog it.
Propagation: seed.

Solanum capsicastrum (winter cherry)

The flowers are small and white with yellow stamens, but it is the berries that follow them that form the decorative feature of this winter pot plant. Leaves are small, pointed and dark green. Stand winter cherries outside during the summer, and

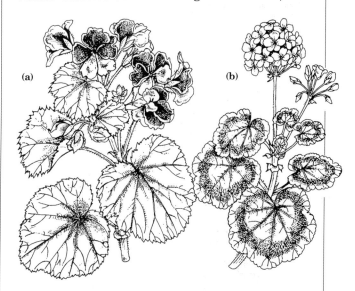

(a)   (b)

Fig. 32 Two popular types of pelargonium. (a) Regals have coarser foliage and larger, frilly flowers than (b) zonals, which have a distinct dark 'zone' on the leaves.

87

The fragrant flowers of the climbing *Hoya carnosa* are almost too perfect to be true – hence the common name of wax plant.

don't forget to water them. The berries can be mildly poisonous, so keep out of the reach of small children.
Light: good light with some direct sun.
Temperature: 10–16 °C (50–60 °F).
Water: keep the compost moist at all times.
Propagation: stem cuttings, seed.

Spathiphyllum wallisii (peace lily)
The flowers are white spathes shielding a creamy white, club-shaped spadix, produced on tall, slender stems. The spathes gradually fade to pale green. Glossy, dark green leaves are lance shaped.
Light: moderate to bright light, out of direct sun.
Temperature: 13–21 °C (55–70 °F).
Water: keep the compost just moist, allowing the surface to dry out between waterings.
Propagation: division.

Stephanotis floribunda (Madagascar jasmine)
A beautiful climber with leathery, dark green, oval leaves on twining stems; the waxy, white, trumpet-shaped flowers are borne in clusters and are very heavily scented. Not an easy plant to grow; it needs constant temperatures and light conditions. Train round a wire hoop for best flowering.
Light: bright light but out of direct sun.
Temperature: 18–21 °C (60–70 °F).
Water: keep the compost constantly moist in spring and summer; allow the surface to dry out between waterings in winter.
Propagation: stem cuttings.

Streptocarpus hybrids (Cape primrose)
Long, strap-shaped, mid-green, rather coarse leaves form a rosette from which tall, dark stems arise carrying heads of flared trumpet-shaped flowers. Flowers may be purple, blue, rose, red, pink or white, often with yellow or white, dark-veined throats. These plants are related to African violets, and like similar conditions.
Light: good light, out of direct sun.
Temperature: 16–21 °C (60–70 °F).
Water: keep the compost just moist, allowing the surface to dry out between waterings. Reduce water in winter.
Propagation: Leaf cuttings, seed, division.

► **Regal pelargoniums have large, almost blowzy flowers.**

·9·
Plants with a Difference

Some indoor plants are a little out of the ordinary – sometimes distinctly exotic. They may be rather more difficult to grow than more common plants, but not necessarily; sometimes they just have very specific needs which are quite easy to cater for. Here are some special groups.

Cacti

Cacti are very popular house plants, probably due to the fact that they will put up with an amazing amount of neglect and remain alive, if not exactly flourishing. They belong to a group known as succulents, which all have fleshy stems or stems and leaves adapted for coping with water shortage.

True cacti do not normally have leaves, but swollen green stems. There are two types: forest and desert cacti. Forest cacti include the well-known Easter and Christmas cactus, and have flattened stems that look like leaves: the desert cacti are the ones that instantly come to most people's minds at the mention of 'cacti'. They may take on a variety of shapes – barrel-shaped and squat, like mammillarias, or tall and cylindrical like the silver torch (cleistocactus) or disc-like, flattened and branching, like opuntias. They generally have round, cushion-like areoles over their surface, from which grow spines or bristles, and flowers and new shoots.

Although cacti are well adapted to drought, this does not mean they will give of their best in drought conditions. Watering needs to be done carefully to avoid rotting of the stems, but it does need to be regular throughout the growing season. Allow the top few centimetres of compost to dry out between each watering, and ensure the compost is gritty and free draining. At the end of the summer, start to reduce the amount of water given, and from autumn to spring, give very little water indeed, just enough to prevent the plants shrivelling.

Desert cacti do need a very light, sunny position; they are some of the few indoor plants that revel in bright, direct sunlight. They do not require high temperatures, however; ordinary room conditions are quite suitable. In winter they should be kept quite cool, between 8° and 15°C (47–60°F).

Some cacti do not flower until they are large, mature plants, and flowers are very unlikely in normal room conditions. Others will flower regularly indoors, given the right treatment. Adequate summer watering and sunlight, plus a cool, dry winter rest, will encourage flowers on suitable varieties. Mammillarias, lobivia, rebutia, notocactus and parodia are not difficult to coax into bloom.

Don't be fooled by the young plants you may see in shops, apparently wreathed in brightly coloured blooms. These are usually artificial flowers stuck into the plants with pins, though this may not be immediately obvious. The pins damage the plants, and encourage rotting.

Food plants

A small number of food crops can be grown indoors, particularly in a conservatory, but also as window-sill plants. They generally need good light, ample watering and regular liquid feeding. Use containers that are as large as practical; growing bags are useful for conservatories, though not particularly decorative.

For the kitchen windowsill, herbs are a must. Not all types will grow well in pots, but parsley, basil, thyme, chervil and marjoram are quite adaptable. Keep growing tips pinched out where necessary to encourage bushiness and remove flower buds as soon as they are seen. It is a good idea to have several pots of each herb; as the ones indoors go past their best they can be cut back fairly hard and put outside to recover while a replacement is brought in.

During their period out of doors, sink the pots in soil to make sure they do not go short of water, and choose a warm, sunny, protected place to position them. In winter you will find supplementary lighting useful to continue the crop.

Several varieties of tomato have been bred with small spaces in mind, and these make good plants for a sunny windowsill, too. Indoors, you will need to pollinate the flowers with a soft brush, and make sure the plants never go short of water. French beans will also give a crop on fairly neat, compact plants, and the globe-rooted varieties of carrots are attractive with their ferny tops. Peppers can be grown very much like tomatoes; 'Redskin' is bred specially with pot growing in mind. The hotter cayenne peppers make very attractive pot plants with their green and red fruits. There are several different types of lettuce that are both attractive and useful. The variety 'Red Salad Bowl' has bronzy, oak-leaf shaped foliage while 'Lollo Rosso' has finely curled and crumpled leaf edges, making a frilly rosette in a pot.

Orchids

Orchids are considered to be among the most exotic of all plants, and there is a great deal of mystique about their culture. They are generally thought to be very difficult to grow, requiring extremely specialized conditions in a hot house. While this may be true of some varieties, there are orchids that can be grown and flowered very successfully indoors with a little care.

Many orchids are epiphytic plants – that is, in their natural habitat they grow on tree branches. In order to store water, they usually have swollen rootstocks which look like bulbs, and are called pseudobulbs. They absorb a lot of their nutrients from the air. They like lightly shaded conditions, and should not be exposed to direct sun. While many species like warm conditions, others will grow happily in normal room temperatures.

Orchids are grown in extremely free-draining composts; it is best to use a specialized orchid compost available from larger garden centres and orchid specialists. Water them regularly with lime-free water in the growing season, but never leave the pots standing in water; after flowering, most orchids have a resting season in which just enough water should be given to prevent the pseudobulbs from shrivelling.

Some orchids that can, with care, be grown in room conditions include cattleya, coelogyne, cymbidium, epidendrum, laelia, miltoni and odontoglossum. For a beginner's orchid, try pleione, a small plant with pink, fringed flowers, or one of the many varieties of miniature cymbidium. Buy from a specialist nursery if possible, where you can obtain good advice on choosing and caring for your plant; orchids are rarely cheap.

Bonsai

These miniature trees originated in Japan, where their training is a highly developed art. Tree

◄ Bonsai trees really belong outdoors, but they can be brought into the home for display for short periods. Many years of careful training go into producing good specimens.

► Many orchids can be grown successfully in the home, despite their exotic appearance. They like humid, lightly shaded conditions. Never allow the pots to stand in water; they must drain freely.

seedlings are selected, potted up and kept artificially small by cultivation techniques that include root pruning and under-potting. Growing tips and branches are carefully trained, often by twisting with wires, so that the tiny tree assumes a gnarled, perhaps windswept appearance: sometimes small glades of two or three trees are grown together. Roots may be trained over pieces of rock to resemble trees growing on a craggy mountainside. In the best examples, which are many years old, the plant looks exactly like a mature tree, but reduced to a fraction of its size.

Our fascination with anything miniature assures the popularity of these trees, but their high price prevents most people from owning one. A good bonsai may easily be 70 years old – 70 years of

careful training and care. There are other specimens that assume a wizened, attractive appearance while still relatively young, however, and these may be affordable though they are hardly ever cheap.

Unfortunately, bonsai are definitely not house plants. Their intricate appearance and high price makes most people want to display them in the home, where they can be appreciated at close quarters, but they are real trees, and real trees just don't grow in indoor conditions. Because part of the technique for keeping them small involves growing them in very shallow dishes, watering is also a problem; they dry out very quickly, and they can also become waterlogged very quickly. A very expensive plant, bought on impulse for the house, can soon become a very expensive mistake.

Bonsai should be grown outside, in a special area which is sheltered from both rain and bright sun. Specimens can be brought indoors for display in rotation, for short periods only. Be prepared to give them individual attention, and learn about their needs.

If you are attracted by bonsai, a cheap way to begin is to take a seedling tree (pines are quite rewarding) and pot it up and train it yourself; there are many specialist books which will tell you how.

Carnivorous plants

In their natural habitat, these plants grow in poor soils, often acid bogs, and obtain extra nutrients by catching and digesting insects. Considered by some gardeners to be rather macabre, they are often interesting rather than beautiful, though they can be very striking and spectacular.

Carnivorous plants have a number of means of trapping their prey. The Venus fly trap, possibly the best known carnivorous plant, has rounded leaves fringed with hairs; when the leaf is stimulated by an insect landing on it, the two

When buying any unusual plant, make sure that you know how to care for it. Ask an assistant for advice, and if possible buy from a specialist nursery. Above all, ensure that you know the full Latin name of the plant, so that you will be able to find out more about it.

sections snap together like a man trap, tightly imprisoning the creature. It is slowly digested, and when the leaf gradually opens once more, only the indigestable debris is left to blow away in the wind. Other plants, such as sundew, have very sticky hairs round the fringes of the leaf; on butterworts the whole leaf surface is sticky. Insects landing on these plants cannot pull themselves away. Yet other plants have long 'pitchers' which contain liquid to drown and digest unwary insects which land in them, having slithered down the inviting slope from the top. Carnivorous plants attract insects by nectar, or sweet scents, or bright colours.

Sphagnum moss is often recommended as a compost for carnivorous plants, though other experts say moss peat with a small amount of Perlite or silver sand added is quite satisfactory. The compost must be acid, and during the spring and summer should be kept saturated; the pot can stand in a dish of water. In autumn, start to reduce the amount of water given until the plants are kept just moist, but not wet, through the winter. Use rainwater rather than tapwater.

Flowers are normally produced in spring, and can be very colourful and attractive – sometimes almost like orchids. Pitcher plants (sarracenia) make particularly fine specimens to grow, and butterworts (pinguicula) and sundews (drosera) are worth cultivating, as well as the Venus fly trap (dionea). Try to buy plants from a specialist nursery.

Index

Page numbers in *italics* indicate an illustration or table.